SNOOZE... OR LOSE!

SNOOZE... OR LOSE!

10 "No-War" Ways to Improve Your Teen's Sleep Habits

HELENE A. EMSELLEM, M.D.

WITH CAROL WHITELEY

Joseph Henry Press
Washington, D.C.

Joseph Henry Press • 500 Fifth Street, NW • Washington, DC 20001

The Joseph Henry Press, an imprint of the National Academy Press, was created with the goal of making books on science, technology, and health more widely available to professionals and the public. Joseph Henry was one of the founders of the National Academy of Sciences and a leader in early American science.

Library of Congress Cataloging-in-Publication Data

Emsellem, Helene.
  Snooze ... or lose : 10 "no-war" ways to improve your teen's sleep habits / by Helene Emsellem and Carol Whiteley.
      p. cm.
  Includes bibliographical references and index.
   ISBN 0-309-10189-1 (hardback) — ISBN 0-309-66021-1 (pdfs) 1. Teenagers—Sleep. 2. Teenagers—Health and hygiene. 3. Sleep deprivation—Health aspects. I. Whiteley, Carol. II. Title.
   RJ496.I6E47 2006
   618.92'8498—dc22
                                   2006011139

Cover image: Getty Images.

Text illustrations: Elaine Robertson.

Printed in the United States of America.

Contents

PART III: WHEN TO SEEK HELP FROM PROFESSIONALS

PART IV: FAMILY AND COMMUNITY SUPPORT

PART V: GLOBAL IMPACTS

Introduction:
Waking Up to the Need for Sleep

To my patients and the medical community, I'm known as a sleep doctor who specializes in teen sleep issues. But at home I'm Mom, and, probably like you, I often see in my family life the negative effects of the sleep issues I deal with every day in my clinic. Living with those effects—and with the teens who experience them—isn't easy, and sometimes it's enough to drive me wild. During the course of raising my three daughters—the youngest, Elyssa, is now in high school— we've had "discussions" about appropriate bedtimes and the need for adequate sleep. There have been *many* frantic mornings trying to get the kids out of bed and out the door and getting my husband and me to work without sending everyone's blood pressure into the danger zone. ("Elyssa, are you up?" "Elyssa, FIVE MINUTES!" "ELYSSA, I'M GOING TO THE CAR NOW AND IF YOU'RE NOT THERE WHEN I START IT YOU'LL BE FINDING YOUR OWN WAY TO SCHOOL!" are the louder and louder exhortations my husband and I have used to clear the house on many mornings.) We have been worried about the kids' health and how well they're learning and frustrated and irritated by living with perpetually sleep-deprived teen zombies.

Does all of this sound familiar? My experiences and my zombies are probably very much like yours—the overwhelming majority of the

11- to 22-year-old set (to which, for the purposes of this book, I refer to as teens or adolescents) simply aren't getting the amount and the quality of sleep they need, and both they and their families are suffering the consequences. But many people think that being sleepy is simply a normal part of being a teen and, despite the epidemic of sleep deprivation, don't consider it a serious issue. We expect teens to be exhausted. We also expect them to be irritable, contentious, and at least a bit zoned out. Being tired and difficult, after all, is just part of being a teen.

That kind of thinking needs to become a thing of the past. The latest research clearly shows that lack of sleep doesn't result just in bleary-eyed youngsters trying to keep from keeling over at the breakfast table. Inadequate sleep, which is anything less than eight and a half hours a nght, can have negative effects—and may have dangerous effects under eight hours—on just about every aspect of teens' lives: their stress level, their grades, their health, their sports performance, their growth, their mood, their emotional stability, their memory, their energy level, their ability to think clearly, their risk of injury, their skin condition, their weight, and their use of drugs and alcohol. Studies have shown that:

- Fifty-five percent of car crashes that result from driver drowsiness are caused by drivers who are 25 or younger.
- Female high school students who go to sleep two or more hours later on the weekend than on weekdays report feeling more depressed than those who don't stay up later on the weekends.
- Students just leaving middle school and beginning high school who sleep less and go to sleep later display more aggressive behavior than those who get more sleep.
- Sleep deprivation increases the likelihood that teens will use nicotine and alcohol.
- Sleepy adolescents react more slowly and have trouble making good decisions.
- Students who receive C's, D's, and F's go to sleep later and have less regular sleep patterns than those who get A's and B's.

• Teens who don't get enough sleep are at higher risk for high blood pressure, diabetes, cancer, heart disease, migraines, and obesity, as well as for suicide and adjustment disorder.

Despite all this evidence, however, most people don't realize that teens—and not just American teens but teens across the globe—are suffering from a huge sleep deficit. When they were babies, they told us, very clearly, when they were exhausted and needed to sleep—they fussed and they wailed and their faces turned red. But now that they're older, our kids don't signal their sleep needs so clearly or so noisily—they often show their extreme fatigue in ways we don't always associate with lack of sleep and do usually attribute to other causes. If they don't do well on an exam, we think it's because they didn't study hard enough. If they're irritating and unpleasant, we blame it on those raging teenage sex hormones. If they gain weight or their skin breaks out, they're not eating a well-balanced diet and not getting enough exercise. If they're unhappy or depressed, well, that's just teenage angst.

Sexual development, cultural forces, diet, and a strong work ethic, as well as a host of other factors, including family problems, physical and psychological conditions, learning issues, heredity, friends, and the environment, do, of course, greatly affect teen behavior, learning, and health. But now the sleep community knows that lack of sleep also underlies, and has an enormous effect on, all parts of teen life and that the right amount and the right kind of sleep are essential for optimum teen well-being.

The sleep community also knows that there's a physiological factor that contributes significantly to teenage sleep deprivation: Teens' brains are actually wired to keep them out of step with most of the world. The secretion of melatonin, a brain hormone that helps cause drowsiness, begins signaling hours later in adolescents than it does in children or adults, turning teens into night owls and making it extremely difficult for them to be awake enough to learn anything during the first few periods of school or to successfully follow a typical adult schedule.

I want to tell you about this critically important finding. And I want you and your family to understand all the ways that lack of sleep is preventing your teenager from doing and being her* best. I also want to help you create an environment that will encourage your teen to get adequate sleep and give you lots of tips and advice on helping your teen take ownership of the sleep issue. In addition, I'm going to tell you how you and your spouse can be good role models when it comes to sleep, a very important part of the program.

If you're at war with your teen over bedtimes and other sleep-related issues, you know that addressing the problems of sleep deprivation can be a challenge—as children of a sleep doc, my kids get more sleep than most, but they need still more and I still have to work hard to convince them that they do. But through my work in my sleep laboratory, my sleep medicine practice, my research studies, and my experiences (good and bad) with my daughters, I've learned a great deal about teen sleep and how to help teenagers get the rest they need. I've packed this book with the latest and most helpful information as well as 10 surefire ways to improve your teen's sleep habits.

I start off with the nitty-gritty: the big reason teens stay up all night and sleep all day, generally driving their parents to distraction. Then I talk about the link between sleep deprivation and serious threats to health and well-being, including high stress, obesity, emotional problems, and increased risk of injury; I devote a separate chapter to the newly understood facts about the direct and critical link between sleep and learning. Then I offer a short primer on sleep itself—what it is, how it works, and why teens need so much of it—and information about the cultural forces and the electronic forces that keep teens from getting the sleep they require.

In the second part of the book you'll find specific tools to help your teen get more and better sleep. A sleepiness scale and a discussion of symptoms kick off the section so your teen can measure and see for herself where she is on the sleep deprivation slope; a scale for adults also is included so you can learn if you too are running on less than

---

*Although sleep deprivation negatively affects teens of both sexes, for brevity's sake I refer to teens throughout the book in the feminine.

adequate sleep and if you need to adopt better sleep habits. Next, my daughter Elyssa and other teenagers provide lots of tips for how to talk with your own teen about the importance of sleep and how you can encourage her—without fighting—to create, follow, and own a realistic sleep program like the one in Chapter 8; that "no-war" program tells you just what teens need to do to feel and be their best. Then, if a bit of additional help is needed, Chapter 9 provides easy-to-follow information on how to reset a stubborn internal sleep-wake clock.

In Part III you'll find information on sleep disorders, including insomnia and sleep apnea, and how to handle the serious problems, including depression, being suicidal, frequent infections, and frequent headaches, that can accompany lack of sleep. I tell you how to recognize the symptoms and where to go for help.

Part IV covers a number of ways you and your community can support your teen's goal of getting more and better sleep. I discuss steps you can take to follow your own healthy sleep program, live a healthy lifestyle, and maintain a supportive home environment. I also talk about what you can do to make your teen's school and community more aware of the dangerous effects of sleep deprivation and how you can encourage your local middle and high schools to move their start times later—a proven way to increase teen learning that's picking up momentum across the United States.

Last but far from least, Part V talks about how the teen sleep problem affects adolescents everywhere and the different ways that cultures around the globe are confronted with—and dealing with—the issue of teen sleep deprivation. The Resources section lists helpful Web sites for additional sleep-related information and memory games to play as well as contact information for locating light therapy products.

Throughout the book you'll also find success stories and advice that I hope will encourage you as you set out to improve your teen's sleep habits and help her optimize her health, learning, and living. In addition you'll find boxes called "A Teen's Take" that give you Elyssa's comments and insight—a teen's point of view—on the subjects being covered; I hope you'll encourage your own teen to read these comments, as well as the rest of the book, to understand and own her sleep issues and patterns.

In all, the book will give you the tools you need to jumpstart and sustain a successful sleep program. But will all the information gathered here make your family's school mornings—and the rest of your days and nights—perfect? In a word, the answer is no. While my husband and I no longer have to shout several times to get Elyssa out the door in the mornings, and she gets enough sleep the night before exams and tries not to sleep all weekend so that her weekdays will be less groggy and her health more assured, occasionally she doesn't get all the sleep she needs. For Elyssa, like most teens, combining all the elements and pressures of her jam-packed day with the perfect night's sleep is a work in progress. But for the most part the sleep program she follows—the one included here—gives her the energy, the attitude, and the ability to do and be her best. I believe that program, plus the additional information and solutions offered in this book, will help you and your teen wake up to the importance of sleep and help your teen get the healthy, success-producing sleep she needs.

Part I

What's Up with Teens?

1

Why Teens Stay Up All Night
and Sleep All Day

When my friend Joan's daughter was in high school, a constant battle raged between her and her mother. Fifteen-year-old Sarah followed a full day of classes with either a piano lesson, a tennis team practice or match, or a meeting of one of the many clubs she belonged to. Then, of course, there was dinner, phoning or IMing friends, working on one of the craft projects she loved to create, watching a little TV, plus hours and hours of homework. Most nights Sarah didn't hit the sheets until midnight at the earliest—and then could barely be roused to make it to school on time the next morning. Joan was more than a little concerned that the five and a half to six hours of sleep Sarah routinely logged wasn't close to the amount she needed and constantly urged Sarah to change her routine and go to bed earlier.

Sarah would have loved to feel less exhausted every school morning, but she enjoyed every one of her activities and refused to give anything up. She also told her mom that even if she wasn't involved in sports and music and clubs and didn't have tons of homework to do, she wouldn't be able to fall asleep any earlier. On the rare evenings when she did have less homework or didn't spend as much time online with her friends, she tried to go to bed a little earlier but nothing happened—she would just lie there getting frustrated until she finally fell asleep close to the usual time. Sarah told her mom that she simply didn't feel tired before midnight or 1:00 in the morning.

Hard as this was for my friend to relate to—Joan herself was so tired in the evenings after working all day at her public relations job, making dinner for her family, helping her younger kids with homework, and doing all the household and family things that needed to be done that day that she was more than ready to collapse by 10:00 p.m.—Sarah wasn't being a stubborn, defiant adolescent (OK, maybe she was being a little stubborn). Like most teenagers, she didn't feel the urge to sleep until well into the night. She would have loved to sleep all morning, and did sleep till close to noon on the weekends, but she just couldn't manage to fall asleep at what her mom considered a reasonable hour.

Does this scenario sound familiar? Most likely it does. I hear similar stories daily in my practice, and I've lived through similar scenarios with my own kids. Teenagers just about everywhere struggle with the negative effects of lack of sleep, but even when their schedule permits it they can't seem to get to sleep early enough to get all that they need before the alarm goes off in the morning. We, as parents, could easily argue that our kids have time-management issues and that they could talk with their friends after school and in the early evening and still have plenty of time to do their homework. But the problem is that they feel most awake, alive, and ready to socialize late at night.

The reason? As we'll talk about in Chapter 5, today's competitive 24/7 world makes it hard for teenagers to turn off and tune out. But a major contributor to most teens' tendency to stay up all night and sleep all day is the chemistry of their brains. Studies show that, while children's and adults' brains are wired to follow a sleep-wake cycle that makes them sleepy in the mid- to late evening and wakeful first thing in the morning, teens' brains signal both sleepiness and wakefulness at much later times.

WHAT'S YOUR TEEN'S NUMBER?

The National Sleep Foundation (NSF) says that adolescents need between eight and a half and nine and a half hours of sleep every night to function optimally but that 85 percent get only six. How many hours of sleep a night does your teen usually get? To see where she falls on the sleep deprivation scale, encourage your teen to take one of the sleepiness tests in Chapter 6 or to keep a sleep log (see Chapter 8) for a week or two.

The Changing Brain

Until recently, scientists believed that the human brain was nearly fully developed by the time its owner reached the age of 3. Babies are born with most of the brain neurons they'll ever have, and unnecessary cells are weeded out during the last several months of gestation. By age 3, it was thought, the brain was pretty much a finished, polished product.

Not so, we now know—the brain continues developing well into the 20s. Dr. Jay Giedd, a neuroscientist at the National Institutes of Health, has led a number of studies that show that the brain undergoes enormous change around the time of puberty, a thinning or "pruning" of neurons, or nerve cells, that doesn't stop until about age 25. Giedd has found that other changes, from a speeding up of neural transmissions to growth in several key areas of the cerebral cortex, occur in the brain as well. From these and others studies, it's clear that the teenage brain is still very much a work in progress.

Part of this ongoing brain development is evidenced in the adolescent tendency to fall asleep and wake up later than other folks. Chemicals in the brain, called neurotransmitters, send and receive messages, some of which signal when it's time to go to sleep and others when it's time to wake up. For example, norepinephrine, dopamine, serotonin, and hypocretin promote alertness and keep the brain awake. Cholinergic transmission is involved in wakefulness and rapid eye movement

A TEEN'S TAKE

❝When I was younger I really, really wished I could stay awake to watch the ball drop on New Year's Eve like everyone else. Then, one summer, I was just able to sleep till 10 in the morning and it was so much easier to stay up at night. Now it's no problem at all. ❞

sleep. Gamma-amino-butyric acid, or GABA, encourages sleep, and melatonin cues winding down in anticipation of sleep. While we are just beginning to understand the highly complex functioning of the sleep-wake cycle at a biochemical level, we do know that it is the dynamic balance of these neurotransmitters in pathways deep in the brain, plus the summary effect they have on a regulatory brain region called the hypothalamus, that puts us at a particular point along the sleep-wake continuum at a particular point in time. Behavior, genetics, light, and the myriad changes associated with puberty also influence the set point for sleep onset.

Children who haven't yet gone through puberty receive these neurochemical sleep-wake signals at times appropriate to, and synchronized with, the day-night cycle. For example, their melatonin production is set in motion in the late afternoon as daylight fades, triggering the onset of the process that eventually produces sleep. Adolescents who have embarked on the puberty trail, however, receive these hormonal signals later in the evening, even though they require the same amount of sleep as their prepubertal friends. Teenagers and younger 20-somethings naturally stay up later because their pineal gland secretes melatonin later, which causes them to fall asleep later than children and adults. Studies done by eminent sleep researcher Mary Carskadon also suggest that the later secretion of melatonin may cause teens to sleep on and on in the morning.

The delayed sleep phase of adolescence.

IDENTIFYING LATER DIM LIGHT MELATONIN ONSET

To determine if kids are receiving their melatonin signals later, it helps to understand where they are in their sexual development. Many doctors make this determination using the Tanner Stages or Tanner Scale (sometimes called the Sexual Maturity Ratings). Developed by pediatric endocrinologist James Tanner, the scale measures the development level of three external sexual characteristics—genital development in boys, breast development in girls, and pubic and body hair distribution in both boys and girls—and provides five stages of development for each characteristic. Stage 1 marks the beginning of puberty for children and Stage 5 signals the attainment of adulthood. The further along in maturation kids are, the more likely they'll be experiencing a delay in sleep onset and the later that delay may become. (If you haven't seen your child streaking through the house lately, it's likely that puberty has at least begun.)

Another way to measure melatonin levels and pinpoint the timing of the sleep cycle is to collect hourly saliva samples from your teen between noon and midnight in a sleep doctor's office. If your teen keeps a careful sleep log for one or two weeks, though, it should provide all the information that's needed to figure out how late the sleep delay is and where the sleep-onset clock is set.

Why do these brain changes occur? Why is melatonin secreted later? We don't really know. But the brain is intricately complex, and the changes it experiences likely benefit the process of maturation in ways we have yet to appreciate. It's also possible that evolution plays a role: Primitive cultures considered pubertal adolescents to be adults, and their ability to stay awake at night to stand watch may have made a valuable contribution to their societies.

For now we only know that in teens the timing of sleep is much later. We also know that the overwhelming majority of young people experience this Delayed Sleep Phase Syndrome, or DSPS, which puts them at odds with the world around them (especially their parents!). It also contributes to making them chronically drowsy and exhausted at times of the day that we think they should be at their peak.

Process S and Process C

To truly understand the adolescent DSPS, you need to understand the biological factors behind it. Two processes—Process S, or the homeostatic sleep system, which refers to the buildup of sleepiness with increasing hours of wakefulness; and Process C, or the human circadian day-night timing system and clock-dependent alertness—are involved in the regulation of the timing of sleep, and both are disturbed in the DSPS. In simple terms, Process S drives the need for sleep and Process C controls the timing of sleeping and wakefulness. How alert or sleepy you are depends on the sum of the interaction of these two processes.

Process S is a pretty straightforward process: The longer you're awake, the greater "sleep need" you accumulate. However, except for a dip in alertness between 2:00 and 5:00 in the afternoon, you don't notice the need to sleep very much until bedtime. That's because it's opposed by powerful circadian clock-dependent alerting signals from a region of the hypothalamus called the suprachiasmatic nucleus (see below). By bedtime, however, the sleep debt is overwhelming and causes you to pull up the comforter for some much-needed ZZZZs.

But what sends our bodies into sleep mode? It's still a bit of a mystery. However, many scientists follow one of two theories: Either a chemical is building up in the brain and when there's enough of it sleep results or a chemical is being depleted in the brain and when it's used up the sleep curtain falls. Whichever is the case, Process S works like a clock, ticking off the time until you get drowsy enough to fall

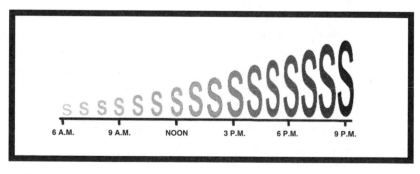

Building sleep debt as the day progresses.

Suppression of the feeling of building sleepiness during the day by Process C: clock-dependent alertness. Note the slight increase in sleepiness at "siesta" time in the later afternoon.

asleep and counting the hours of sleep necessary to restore energy and alertness.

The problem with Process S and teens, though, is that teens don't get as sleepy as quickly as adults and younger kids do; the curve for how sleepy teens get actually slows down and teens don't accumulate as many "sleepiness points" as their younger siblings or parents. So a 15-year-old going through puberty can be up for the same number of hours as a 10-year-old or a 40-year-old but not feel as sleepy. That makes feeling awake well into the wee hours much easier for teens, but they still need nine hours of sleep to discharge their sleepiness.

Superimposed on this pattern lies the workings of Process C, in which our internal body clock regulates all of our biological processes. Process C causes us to feel more alert at certain times of the day even if, according to Process S, we've been awake long enough to have gained a large number of sleepiness points.

Our internal body clock is actually centered in a pinhead-sized nucleus called the suprachiasmatic nucleus, or SCN, that is deep in the hypothalamic region of the brain and receives environmental information about daylight and darkness via the retina. When that information

Children

Adolescents

Later onset of alertness and slower accumulation of sleep need in adolescence.

is relayed to the SCN by way of the retino-hypothalamic pathway, the hypothalamus establishes body process patterns in accordance with the day-night cycle. Those processes include brain wave activity, hormone production, cell regeneration—and sleeping and waking times.

In teens, however, Process C is set to a later clock time, enabling them, as we well know, to sleep late in the morning even though it's light outside. While Process C causes most adults to experience robust alertness during the day and the strongest need for sleep between 2:00 a.m. and 4:00 a.m., teens' sleep phase delay causes their strongest dip in alertness to be between 3:00 and 7:00 a.m. and can make that dip last until 9:00 or 10:00 a.m. if the teens are sleep deprived. If it's hard

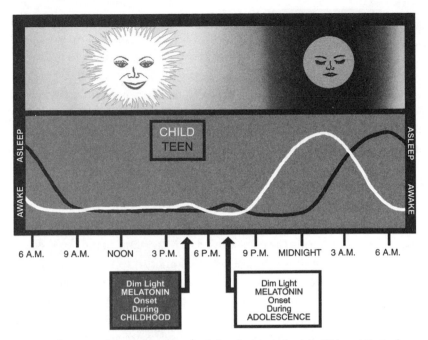

CHILD
TEEN

| 6 A.M. | 9 A.M. | NOON | 3 P.M. | 6 P.M. | 9 P.M. | MIDNIGHT | 3 A.M. | 6 A.M. |

Dim Light
MELATONIN
Onset
During
CHILDHOOD

Dim Light
MELATONIN
Onset
During
ADOLESCENCE

Contrast between the sleep-wake schedule of a prepubertal child and that of an adolescent. Specifically note the later onset of alertness, later dim light melatonin onset signaling the initiation of processes leading to sleep, and later sleep onset time for the teen.

to understand why it's so incredibly difficult to wake a sleeping teen at 6:00 a.m., think how hard it would be if you had to get up for work at 3:00 a.m.—it's pretty much equivalent.

For sleep to occur, the clock-dependent alertness that's generated by Process C needs to be turned off by melatonin. For children and adults who go to bed at 10:00 p.m., melatonin secretion, or dim light melatonin onset, typically begins about six hours earlier, around 4:00 p.m. But in adolescents melatonin onset may not occur until hours later.

Still another problem is the length of the day. Children's and adults' body clocks follow a day that is approximately 24.3 hours long, but— you guessed it—the adolescent body clock beats to a different drum. Teens' biological processes work to a slightly longer day, one that can last up to 24.7 hours. Their longer day makes it even easier for them to sleep late in the morning, especially when they're sleep deprived.

All of this means trouble for teens. Because their day-night cycle doesn't follow the typical 24-hour clock, they don't make the day-night shift when everyone else does—their morning comes later and their day lasts longer. And because they typically need to follow the schedule adults adhere to, they feel out of whack and are always trying to cram a longer day into a 24-hour period—and suffering the consequences. Alterations of the three sleep-wake factors—the slower buildup of sleepiness during the day, the delayed influence of light, and the longer day—make our adolescents different and uncomfortably out of sync.

Teens' sleep phase shift desynchronizes them from the 24-hour day that the circadian rhythm is entrained, or geared, to—in other words, it upsets the balance between teens' timing for sleeping and waking and the timing of what's going on in their environment. And as they progress through puberty and go to sleep later and later, becoming sleep deprived from having to get to school so early in the morning, they desynchronize even further and become true night owls. Without intervention and treatment to put teens back in sync, their circadian

Physiologic and social pressures resulting in a restricted total sleep time.

Another Teen Says . . .

❝I don't like being a night owl. It makes it very hard for me to maintain a normal schedule and I feel like I miss so much—mornings, breakfast, a lot of daytime productivity, classes, relationships. Now that I'm working I'm missing out on the opportunity to make a good impression by showing up early—or even on time.**❞**

---

clocks get pushed out so late at night that they fail to put them to sleep at anything like a normal hour.

Catching Up—Or Staying Behind?

With their changing, out-of-sync brain chemistry, and suffering from the phase shift that results, is it any wonder that teenagers are often out of sorts and out of energy? On the one hand, their bodies are telling them to go to sleep at midnight or even later, and on the other hand society is telling them they have to get up early to go to school. The physiological demands of adolescence are daunting enough on their own—and starting earlier and earlier (girls, on average, now get their first period at the age of 11)—without the negative effects of sleep deprivation and the added demands that lack of sleep puts on the body.

So what do most teens do to counter that feeling of total exhaustion and to help them make it through their school-, sports-, family-, and activity-filled weeks? Well, they sleep till noon on the weekends, of course, trying to catch up on as much sleep as they can beyond the five or six hours that is the norm on school nights.

But that's not a solution. In fact, in the long run, catching up by sleeping late on the weekends actually causes more problems. If teens get up at noon on Sunday, they'll need to accumulate sleepiness for 15 or 16 hours before they can go to sleep again—which means they may not be able to fall asleep until 4:00 a.m. on Monday! The late weekend wake-up time only reinforces the underlying sleep phase delay. It also makes it hard for teens to fall asleep at a reasonable time on Sunday night and causes them to be significantly sleep deprived come Monday morning. By sleeping late teens may feel better because they've paid

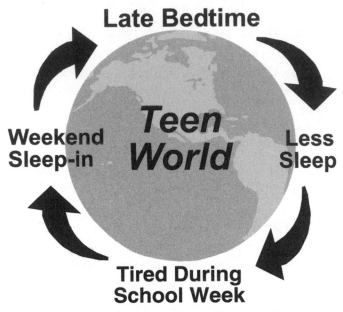

Adolescent vicious cycle of sleep deprivation and late sleep-ins on weekends perpetuating the delay in sleep phase.

back some of their sleep debt, but at the same time they're perpetuating the desyncronization between their day-night cycle and their school schedule.

The NSF agrees that sleeping late on the weekends is not a solution to sleep problems. It reports that irregular sleep schedules, which include those with major differences in the time and duration of sleep between weekdays and the weekend, further contribute to a shift in sleep phase. Not only that, but irregular sleep patterns result in difficulty falling asleep or waking up and in poor sleep quality. These problems can produce teens who not only stay just as exhausted as ever but who suffer a whole raft of emotional, behavioral, physical, and health problems.

Can sleep-deprived kids ever really catch up? Without getting their circadian rhythm back on track, the answer is probably not. Think of it this way. Say, your daughter gets to bed around midnight on a routine basis. She's got to catch the 6:30 bus to get to school for the 7:20 start time, which means she drags herself into the shower at about 6:15. Most weekdays she barely gets six hours of sleep—which is at least three hours less than the nine-plus hours teens need to function optimally. So over the course of a school week, your daughter is deprived of 15 hours of all-important sleep.

Then, let's say, she sleeps from 1:00 a.m. to noon on both Saturday and Sunday. Ah, you think, she's catching up, she's getting her much-needed nine hours on both days plus two extra hours. But we have to look at the big picture. Yes, she's getting more sleep than she does on school nights, but since she needs nine hours, she's only paying back two hours of sleep debt each night. Even after a great weekend of sleep, your daughter is still deprived of nearly 11 hours of the good stuff—and that's after only one week of school!

Being so significantly sleep deprived causes problems. (Getting a bit less than nine hours a night on occasion may not have a major negative impact on your teen's well-being, but chronic sleep restriction of less than eight hours a night has been proven to impair it.) What are those problems? Everything from being downright grouchy and more than a little unpleasant to health problems, including a higher risk for infections and obesity; emotional problems, such as increased anger and sadness; judgment problems, including the inability to think clearly; increased risk of injury; poorer sports performance; and an increased propensity to abuse alcohol and other drugs. In the following chapter I'll go into depth on these and other problems related to sleep deprivation, and in Chapter 4 you'll find an in-depth look at the newly discovered, critical link between learning and sleep. In both chapters you'll learn how sleep deprivation is a major threat to your teen's well-being.

2

The Real Reason Teens Are Tired, Low Performing, Stressed, Overweight, and Incredibly Hard to Live With

If your child, around the age of 12, 13, or 14, became someone you no longer recognized, you're not alone. Many children, when they reach adolescence, make a sudden transformation from little darling to big challenge as they become more irritable, more socially conscious, more moody, and more stressed. They may also do less well at school and never have the energy for anything other than closing themselves in their room to listen to music or IM their friends.

Adolescence can certainly be a time of change and frustration—for both the teens going through it and their parents. You, like many parents, may be mourning the loss of that sunny-dispositioned kid who was always ready to go for a bike ride with the family and who thought math was really cool—and may need to learn how to relate to the new incarnation. But teens, too, go through significant changes: Along with the physiological demands of the age—shooting up several inches, growing beards or breasts, developing more muscle—they are changing and growing emotionally, socially, and behaviorally. All of that change—as we know only too well—can make them tired, grumpy, and even a bit irrational. And because we see so many tired and grumpy teens around us, we usually assume that's the normal state of affairs for this age group.

It's definitely true that across-the-board change can cause teens to look and act in less than stellar ways. But recent studies have shown that it's not only adolescence itself that throws teens—and their families—into a tailspin. Underlying the exhaustion and the irritability, and adding or aggravating a whole slew of other conditions, is sleep deprivation.

What would teens be like if they weren't continually sleep deprived? If they could get a good night's sleep night after night, would there be happier, healthier, more energetic, and better-performing youngsters sitting across from us at the dinner table? All signs point to yes. (OK, they'd still be wearing those enormous baggy pants and the spaghetti-strap tank tops with their bellies showing—unfortunately getting enough rest doesn't solve teen fashion issues.) In simple terms, lack of sleep and being sleep phase delayed make a challenging time of life much harder to cope with by robbing teens of what their bodies need to refresh, repair, fight off damaging physical and emotional conditions, and grow.

> **SNOOZE NEWS**
>
> While you might think that the common cold would be considered one of the greatest afflictions affecting Americans, author Nancy Stedman, in researching her article "Tired of Being Tired?", found that it is actually drowsiness that bedevils the most people.

But problems don't arise just from sleepiness—there's another side to the sleep deprivation issue. When you're sleeping less, you have to sustain wakefulness longer, and this puts extra stress on your body, which leads to additional problems. Think of it this way: If you're getting only six hours of sleep, your body has to stay awake for 18 hours—which is nearly impossible to do at peak functionality. It's very difficult for a human being to sustain wakefulness for 18 or more hours at a clip.

When does functionality drop off? The critical point of dysfunction appears to be when you hit between 15 and 16 hours of cumulative sleep loss. So if your teen is sleeping only five hours a night, when she should be getting more than nine, after four nights (four hours' loss per night times four nights) functionality will be at a less than optimal level. And that decreased functionality applies across the board—in school performance, emotional stability, behavior, ability to fight off infection, you name it.

SOME IS THE SAME AS NONE

In a recent experiment on sleep deprivation, the participants, who were in their early 20s, were divided into four groups. Group 1 volunteers slept for four hours per night over a two-week period, Group 2 volunteers slept for six hours, Group 3 members slept for eight hours, and Group 4 members had no sleep at all for three days straight. At the end of the two weeks, those who had slept for eight hours a night functioned well—no surprise there. But the big surprise was that there was no difference in performance level between those who had slept four or six hours for two weeks and those who had not slept at all for three days. The experiment showed that adolescents cannot perform well without any sleep but also that they can't perform well with much less than the nine hours they require.

The Impact of Sleep Deprivation

What exactly is less than optimal performance? Is it really all that bad? As you'll see in the following sections, statistics show that chronic sleep deprivation puts teens in a blunted, muted "slough state," severely reducing their ability to learn, behave, and live at their best.

Health Issues

Lack of sleep impacts teens' physical health in several different ways. For one, it impairs their immune system, interfering with their white blood cells' ability to fight off infection in the bloodstream; experiments have shown that once in sleep debt the body's number of T cells decreases by 30 to 40 percent. That suggests that sleep-deprived teens are much more likely to catch the colds, flus, and other acute and chronic illnesses that seem to be permanent inhabitants of most high schools and teen activity centers. And that of course means they'll be missing classes and sports events, with all that entails, feeling crummy and worn out, and behaving even more like bears than ever. It could also mean they're more susceptible to catching potentially serious viruses or developing intercurrent, or coexisting, illnesses.

Once tired teens come down with a cold or flu, their compromised immune system may also cause the condition to hang on longer. The National Commission on Sleep Disorders Research warns that sleep

In a National Institutes of Health study, rats were deprived of sleep to see what the effects would be. One group of rats was continually deprived of REM sleep (for information about REM sleep, see Chapter 3). A second group was deprived of all sleep. Rats normally live for two to three years, but those that were allowed no REM sleep lived for only five weeks. The rats denied all sleep lived for only three weeks.

The cause of their greatly shortened life spans? Sleep deprivation in animals produces a condition that eventually becomes lethal. Completely sleep-deprived animals develop a syndrome of hypothalamic dysfunction: They overeat, lose weight, lose hair, develop skin lesions, and eventually die of infection. However, researchers have discovered that the syndrome is reversible with sleep—studies suggest that sleep restores the immune system and the antioxidant balance.

deprivation can be "a significant barrier to recovery, potentially exacerbating a primary illness." So a bug that a rested teen could fight off in two or three days might stay around for four or five. And once the virus is finally gone, it's very likely to come back; sleep deprivation also contributes to recurring and chronic conditions. That cough your teen just never seems to be able to shake could be the result of her ongoing sleep deficit. (It could also be the result of allergies or asthma, which also are associated with sleep deprivation.)

In addition to catching more colds and flus, sleep-deprived teens have a higher rate of headaches. Often kids show up at my clinic complaining of headaches and sometimes severe migraines. Because puberty is a peak time for the onset of migraines, many of these kids want medication to relieve the pain. But it often turns out, after consultation and testing, that these teens simply need more sleep, not a drug. When rested, their incidence of migraines may drop dramatically and tension headaches disappear.

A 15-year-old patient of mine I'll call Henry came to me complaining of severe and frequent headaches. The headaches had gotten so bad that Henry, who was an honor student, had been missing a lot of school. He was worried about being able to keep up with classes and the school was concerned about his absenteeism. Finally, a school administrator contacted the family, who contacted their family doctor. But the doctor wasn't able to find the cause of the headaches and sent Henry to a neurologist. Complicating the already confusing situation was the fact that Henry's mother suffered from migraines, so everyone he saw had looked for a link.

Months went on, with Henry trying four different migraine medications that the neurologist prescribed. But the headaches improved only minimally both in terms of frequency and severity and continued starting up within an hour of Henry's waking up. He was getting no relief and often missed morning classes. When he did make it to school on time he generally wound up in the nurse's office, too sick to finish the day.

After determining that the migraine medications were not helping to the extent they should have, the astute neurologist thought that lack of sleep might be causing the problem. He referred Henry to my office, and after testing and consultation, it turned out that Henry was severely sleep deprived. On most weeknights he would get into bed sometime around 11:00 but then just lie there until close to 1:00, unable to fall asleep. When he finally nodded off, it was only a little more than five hours until his alarm started blaring at him to get to school on time. And by the time he got out of the shower, another splitting headache had developed.

Once I found that Henry had a major sleep phase delay, I started him on a course of treatment. The first step for him, and for all my patients, was education. I sat down with Henry and his parents and talked about sleep: its phases, its requirements, the changes in patterns associated with adolescence, and particularly why Henry was feeling so awful and needed to get more sleep—his brain was running late but his school was starting early. I also told him how my staff and I were going to help him.

It all came as a surprise. Like many teens and their parents, Henry and his folks had no idea that teens need at least nine hours of sleep to function at their best and that their sleep-wake cycle is wired to be out of sync with everything around them. But Henry was so medically ill by the time I saw him that the news was welcome—at last he had found some help.

Because Henry was so sick, and because adjusting the sleep-wake cycle can take several weeks, I contacted his school to make a change in his schedule immediately. An elective class, on photography, that Henry took started at 7:30, and a reluctant Henry—who loved the class and wanted to do it all—accepted my recommendation to drop the course in order to start school a period later. When his parents contacted the administrators about making the change, they agreed to do so after receiving a letter from me confirming the need. (A note here: Most schools are generally compliant about making these kinds of adjustments when they're presented with a carefully written letter from the treating physician, but no school will change every teen's schedule, so schedule changes are best saved for teens who need immediate relief from pain or illness. To learn what you can do to have all middle and high schools in your area start later in the morning, see Chapter 13.) Dropping a favorite subject was a tradeoff for Henry, a compromise, but the headaches were making him sick and miserable and my staff and I finally convinced him that he could take the elective the following semester, after his sleep deficit and headaches were under control.

A TEEN'S TAKE

❝After a long hard week of school, sports, and homework, all I want to do is talk to my friends and have some 'me' time. But on the weekends I generally have a very early tennis match, which means I have to get up at 6:00 a.m. to get to a tournament on time. There's always just so much to do. ❞

How quickly did that control come about? Treating kids with severe sleep deprivation and delayed sleep phase is generally at least a six- to eight-week process requiring continuing reenforcement. But because of the schedule change, Henry was immediately able to start sleeping 45 minutes later in the morning, making a big difference in the severity of his headaches and making him feel a whole lot better. However, the schedule change didn't address Henry's underlying delayed sleep phase, so in addition to eliminating his first-period class I recommended that Henry increase the amount of light he got in the

LIGHT BOXES AND LIGHT VISORS

A successful way to help push your teen's sleep-wake cycle into a more normal pattern is to have her wear a light visor for 20 minutes in the morning; the visor's intense light will reinforce a normal wake-up time. A light box will also increase the light cues your youngster receives, but to use a light box your teen will need to get up 20 minutes earlier to sit in front of it— which can be counterproductive during the school week. A light visor can be worn easily while getting dressed and ready for class. (To learn more about treating sleep deprivation with light boxes and light visors, see Chapter 9. For information on where to purchase these products, see Resources at the end of the book.)

morning through the use of a light box or light visor (you probably recall from Chapter 1 that teens are not influenced as strongly as adults by light and that they're able to sleep well into the morning even though the sun is shining). By taking in more light, Henry would reinforce his wake-up time and get his internal clock back on track, so that he could wake up at a reasonable time in the morning and fall asleep more readily by 11:00 at night. Bright light is the most powerful stimulus for shifting the timing of sleep.

How did the combined treatment work? As Henry said, his headaches gradually diminished, but he reported after two weeks that he wasn't falling asleep much earlier. However, he did say that he felt far more awake and energetic in the daytime. And that's a typical response. Often, before kids notice any greater ease in falling asleep, they realize they're feeling a little better and have more energy during the day.

After several more weeks things usually start improving noticeably; they did for Henry. Within two months his headaches subsided greatly, and by using a light visor and managing his wake-up time his sleep-wake cycle started to shift and he was able to fall asleep earlier. By the following semester he was feeling well enough to go back to a full-time schedule—and take that photography class.

During the summer, however, Henry got out of sync again because he let his cycle slip back into a delayed sleep phase—school was out and he stayed up later with his friends. But he had to get to his summer

One Patient Says . . .

❝ *Lack of sleep has made keeping up with everything at school much more difficult. I found myself missing school at least once a week—I just couldn't get out of bed because I had slept so little on previous days. Even more problems ensued when I developed an inflammation in my digestive system [for more on the link between lack of sleep and digestive problems, see below]. I was sick for months and missed school just about every other day—every time I thought I was better I was out of school again, and that hurt my social life as well as my schoolwork. So little sleep made me completely sick and stressed.* **❞**

---

job by 8:00 a.m.—and guess what? His headaches returned and he felt exhausted again. But this time Henry knew what to do, and he didn't wait until the problem was entrenched before he solved it. He got back on a schedule, limited his late nights, and started using his light visor again. Things weren't perfect—teens do love their late nights, for privacy and for communicating with friends—but the treatment made Henry feel much, much better and enabled him to function a lot more comfortably. (For more on the sleep deprivation–headache link, see Chapter 11.)

Incidence of Injury

Insufficient sleep can dramatically increase your teen's risk of injury and death, particularly while driving a car. According to the National Highway Traffic Safety Administration, drowsiness or fatigue is a major cause of at least 100,000 police-reported traffic crashes each year that kill more than 1,500 Americans and injure 71,000. Drivers under the age of 25 are responsible for 55 percent of those accidents.

One state, New Jersey, has enacted a law that classifies drowsy driving—defined as operating a motor vehicle after having been awake for 24 hours or longer—in the same category as drunk driving, making those convicted eligible for second-degree homicide charges. The law, called Maggie's Law, named after Maggie McDonnell, a 20-year-old college student who was killed by a drowsy driver who had been awake for 30 hours, was enacted in 2003. In 2005 the first driver, a New

Jersey resident who killed another driver because of sleepiness and inattention, was jailed under the law.

Why do young drivers in the United States cause so many crashes? Certainly lack of driving experience plays a role. But it is being sleepy—most teenagers' chronic state—that contributes significantly to the potentially deadly mistakes they make behind the wheel. And according to sleep researcher Mary Carskadon, similar negative effects on functioning are found in people who live in the rest of North America and in industrialized countries on other continents.

The American Academy of Pediatrics tells us that sleeping six to seven hours a night is associated with a 1.8 times higher risk for involvement in a sleep-related crash compared to sleeping eight or more hours. Sleeping less than five hours a night presents a 4.5 times higher risk. Studies analyzing motor vehicle crash data report that 40 percent of drivers who fell asleep at the wheel and crashed had been awake for 15 or more hours and that nearly 20 percent had been awake for 20 or more hours.

Being sleepy while driving is also strongly associated with brief mental lapses, which of course can be deadly if you're speeding down the highway and you blank out for even a few seconds. It also makes it difficult to stick with certain types of behavior, especially routine or boring ones, such as holding the steering wheel in one position while you dazedly watch the road go by. Tiredness also greatly reduces visual reaction time, which might prevent drivers from avoiding an obstacle that suddenly appears in the road, as well as auditory reaction time, which might keep drivers from realizing that the driver of the car they're about to hit is honking the horn at them.

> **SNOOZE NEWS**
>
> About 1 million, or one-sixth of, traffic crashes in the United States are believed to be caused by a lapse in driver attention. Sleep loss and exhaustion increase the chances of such a lapse.

Sleep deprivation also decreases the ability to remember and think clearly, which means that exhausted teen drivers could forget the speed limit or be unable to find the best way home after taking a few wrong turns. (I'll talk more about the negative effects sleepiness has on these factors in Chapter 4, "The Sleep-Learning Link.")

If your teen drives drowsy, the evidence shows that the risk of injury or death rises to a great degree. And teens do drive drowsy: More than half the adolescent drivers who participated in the National Sleep Foundation's 2006 Sleep in America poll say they had driven drowsy during the past year, and 15 percent of participating 10th- to 12th-grade drivers report driving drowsy once a week. But feeling sleepy isn't the only issue—increased awake time, reduced sleep time, and the phase of your teen's internal body clock are all independent risk factors for drowsy-driving accidents. That means that teens are at risk of having an accident if they sleep only six hours at night and drive to school when they should still be in their sleep cycle as well as when they're driving home at night after they've been awake for 18 hours. Dr. Christian Guilleminault, an international sleep expert, studied the effects of sleep deprivation in the laboratory and extrapolated his findings to real-life situations on the open road in France. He concluded that road safety campaigns should encourage drivers to avoid driving after sleep deprivation even on relatively short trips, especially if they feel sleepy.

Is your child safe because she is a very good driver? Unfortunately it's not only "bad" kids who drag race or take chances behind the wheel who suffer the consequences. Sleep researcher Mary Carskadon found that high school boys who have the most extracurricular time commitments were the most likely to report falling asleep at the wheel; a hard-working male teen who plays sports after school and then works at a job in the evening may be at the greatest risk of a fatal fatigue-related motor vehicle accident. Crashes can happen to any teen who isn't getting enough sleep.

They are also more likely to happen if a sleep-deprived teen driver drinks alcohol. Banks et al. studied the relationship between age, alcohol, sleep deprivation, and crash risks. After evaluating 20 healthy volunteers with an average age of 23, they found that alcohol, even at legal blood concentrations (under 0.08 in most states), increased sleepiness and impaired both performance and the ability to detect crash risks when the volunteers had been restricted to five hours of sleep.

Teens, though, don't need to drink and drive to have impaired performance. Other studies have shown that sleep deprivation produces psychomotor response (responses that involve both the brain

WATCH FOR THESE SIGNS

Encourage your teen, and anyone else who drives, to read through this list of danger signs prepared by the National Sleep Foundation to help prevent trouble on the road:

- Feeling the need to turn up the radio or roll down the window
- Having difficulty focusing or keeping your eyes open
- Yawning repeatedly
- Having wandering, disconnected thoughts
- Feeling restless or irritable
- Drifting out of your lane or hitting the shoulder strips
- Tailgating or missing traffic signs or exits

If your teen experiences any of these signs, it's time for her to get off the road; find a safe, well-lit place for a 20-minute nap; or call someone to pick her up.

and movement) impairments—including the ability to stay in your own lane—equivalent to those caused by consuming alcohol at or above the legal limit. After teens are awake for more than 16 hours, they drive as though they had a blood alcohol level of 0.05 to 0.1 percent.

To see where your teen stands in her ability to drive safely, encourage her to take one of the interactive video tests—the Reaction Test Challenge, the Interactive Hazard Perception Test, or the Drunk Driving Test— offered online at *www.steerclear.org.uk.* Click the "Interactive" button on the home page to bring up the choice of tests.

Using Equipment and Playing Sports

Just as sleepiness impairs a person's ability to drive a car or a truck, it also impairs teens' use of other mechanical equipment. Tools that require care and thought to operate, like jigsaws in shop class or lawnmowers in after-school or summer

SNOOZE NEWS

In many jurisdictions, the forms that police officers complete at the scene of a traffic accident have now been updated to include questions about the amount of sleep the driver has had. In the last few years more attention has finally been paid to the link between age, sleep deprivation, and accident rates, which has resulted in uncovering the fact that teenagers are overrepresented in fatigue-related crashes.

gardening jobs, can be extremely hazardous if handled by a sleep-restricted user. In my practice I always caution teen patients to stay away from dangerous equipment and to not drive until their sleep debt is paid off. When sleep deprived they just can't think clearly enough or react fast enough to use machinery safely.

Sleepiness can also increase teens' risk of sports injuries. Just as they can suffer an attention lapse on the road or while using a power tool, they can tune out for a few seconds and run into another player or get hit by a bat or stick because they're not attentive to their surroundings. Reduced reaction time can also make it difficult to avoid being hit by a wild pitch or to sidestep an obstacle. And, of course, sleep-deprived players won't be able to perform anywhere near their best. A recent study of aces and winning serves on a tennis team showed evidence of a strong link between serving aces and having adequate sleep. Another study, led by a researcher at the University of Chicago Medical School, found that after only a week of sleep deprivation, men ages 18 to 27 metabolized glucose (sugar) less efficiently and had elevated levels of cortisol, a stress-related hormone. Glucose is the main source of energy for athletes and elevated cortisol levels have been linked with impaired physical recovery.

Weight Gain and Obesity

Though it may seem counterintuitive, the less you sleep, the more weight you gain. You might think that being awake longer would help you burn more calories, keeping weight from piling on, but in reality not getting enough sleep makes it more likely you'll become obese. That's because sleep loss decreases the level of hormones called leptins, which tell the body its full, and increases the level of ghrelin hormones, which trigger the appetite to pick up. When you're sleep deprived you feel hungry and you can eat more than you should. On the other hand, getting more sleep actually supports metabolism and has a protective effect against obesity.

SNOOZE NEWS

The word "leptin" comes from the Greek word "leptos," meaning thin. Leptins are produced by fat cells and circulate in the bloodstream. They signal the brain when you've eaten enough and it's time to stop.

Studies of overweight and obese patients indicate that they sleep less than their thinner counterparts. According to the North American Association for the Study of Obesity, people who get 10 or more hours of sleep are 11 percent *less* likely to become obese. Those who sleep six hours a night are 23 percent *more* likely to become obese and those who get five hours of sleep are 50 percent more likely to be obese. The exhausted folks who log only four or fewer hours a night are 73 percent more likely to be obese than those who get adequate rest.

Sleep researcher James Gangwisch reports that the relationship between sleep and obesity applies to children and adolescents as well as adults. A recent study of 12 young men linked the reduction in leptin associated with sleep loss to increased hunger and appetite, especially for high-calorie, high-carbohydrate foods. And we all know that exhausted teens who need to live by society's schedule often survive on fat-filled fast food because they don't have the time to eat lower-calorie, well-balanced meals. If your teen is overweight, more exercise and less eating are certainly in order. But a good night's sleep, night after night after night, may also contribute to a healthier, fitter body and the prevention of a lifetime of obesity—which in turn can prevent depression, to which obesity is often linked. Adequate sleep can also lower the risk for diabetes, which increases with weight gain and with the body's inability to metabolize sugar properly. In addition it can help to prevent sleep apnea, a sleep disorder that can accompany obesity. (For more on the link between sleep loss and diabetes, see Chapter 11; for more on the connection between sleep loss and sleep apnea, see Chapter 10.)

Irritability and Mood Swings

OK, I know—it's already very clear to you that teens can be moody beings. You've seen your daughter swing more than once from an exuberant high to grouchy prickliness to barely conversant back to excited and alive. The many changes of adolescence can make teenagers emotional and volatile, and they can also be easily wounded and much more fragile than they appear. Even when they're well rested, teens can leap up and down the emotional scale. When they're sleep deprived, their emotions can tend toward the negative side and be much harder for them to control.

❝Mood swings are probably one of the worst parts of being a teenager. Sometimes you feel yourself just being pissed off for no apparent reason. Then you can be laughing with your friend on the phone and the next minute you hear a song that reminds you of something sad and suddenly you're in a terrible mood. It sucks, but you just can't control it. ❞

According to the American Academy of Pediatrics, adolescents who have sleep problems report increased negative moods and/or trouble regulating their moods. And looking at it from the opposite direction, adolescents with clinical mood disorders report high rates of sleep disturbances. While stress may contribute to sleep problems and emotional volatility (see below), there is solid evidence that sleep loss and irregular sleep patterns can make teens irritable and moody.

Stress can make teens' lives very difficult indeed. For example, they might surprise themselves—and everyone around them—by getting angry over a situation that, when they're well rested, they might shrug off. Or they might become aggressive when they're driving because they get excessively irritated when another driver cuts in front of them. A sad scene in a movie might make them unhappy and down for hours. And a disagreement with a friend could easily turn into a major blowup. A study using a standard measure of moods, called the Profile of Mood States, showed that restricted sleep time adversely affects all aspects of mood, from anxiety to dejection to anger to vigor to inertia to confusion.

Why can sleepy teens feel not only out of sync but also out of sorts? Sleep loss alters the activity of neurotransmitters produced in the brain that regulate emotions. With these changes, we feel emotions more intensely and have greater trouble coping with them. And that can lead to even more difficult and serious conditions. Kids who can't control their emotions might feel there's something really wrong with them and become depressed and even suicidal (see Chapter 11 for more on the link between sleep loss and clinical depression). Or they might turn to drugs or alcohol in an attempt to lessen the strong feelings they're experiencing. They might be too upset or angry and disruptive to do well in school. And any form of emotional upheaval they go through could lead them to get even less rest, which could result in greater and long-term health and behavioral problems.

Memory

Memory is involved in just about everything we do. We need to remember how to get home, what to pick up at the grocery store, the formula for figuring out how many yards of carpeting we need for the living room, and where in the world we left the car keys *this* time. For teens, memory is just as important: They have to remember their homework assignments, the plays for the next football game, which day the SAT will be given, and where in the world they left the car keys *this* time. A highly functioning memory is critical to performing and living at our best.

In simple terms, sleep deprivation interferes with memory function. In fact, studies show that it has a dramatically negative effect not only on memory formation but on memory access and retrieval. A sleep-deprived brain keeps neurons from firing quickly enough and working smoothly and efficiently enough to provide you with the information you need in a reasonable time.

Memory function fails when a teen, who needs around nine hours of sleep nightly, chronically gets only six to seven. And that failure is pervasive—it affects the teen's ability not only to remember facts and figures but to sort things out and think clearly. Sleep loss particularly affects episodic memory, that is, your memory time and spatial relationship—what you need to answer the questions on a history quiz. French researchers have found a clear association between restricted REM sleep time (see Chapter 3 for information about REM sleep) and episodic memory deficits when adolescents were given a "what, where, when"–type test.

A strongly functioning memory, then, is key to learning and to doing well in school. And because teens spend so much of their life in school and learning all sorts of things, I've continued this section on memory in another chapter that's devoted entirely to learning. See Chapter 4, "The Sleep-Learning Link," for a comprehensive look at this all-important topic.

Energy Level

It doesn't take a rocket scientist—or a neurologist—to tell you that when you're tired, you have no energy. But being sleep deprived doesn't just make you feel like crawling to the nearest couch and staying there. Chronic sleep loss produces a global decrease in energy, so you think, move, and react more slowly. Without enough rest, your body doesn't have the time it needs to repair and restore itself, so everything you do is done at only a percentage of your top speed and effectiveness.

When you're exhausted, do you have the energy you need to put in the hours to finish a big project? Do you feel up to tackling chores or even having a night out with your spouse or friends? Your teen feels the same way. When she is tired, doing anything can seem impossible. That includes exercising—and not exercising, like other negative effects of sleep loss, can have several negative effects of its own. For one, it can lead to weight gain—tired teens are much more likely to ask for a ride to school than walk or bike, and to take the elevator rather than the stairs. They'll drag their way through gym class and probably choose not to go out for a sport; if they do, their reduced reaction time and unclear thinking will increase their likelihood of injury. If they do gain a lot of weight, they may be more unhappy or depressed, not to mention unhealthy. And because exercise is a good stress reducer, lack of energy can make teens' stress level shoot up. For teens who tend toward being anxious to begin with, their stress level can skyrocket.

A Case History and a Study

Anna (I've changed all patients' names to keep them anonymous) was a patient who had been tired and lacking energy for years. In the second semester of her junior year of high school she finally told her parents that she was sick and tired of being sick and tired and asked them to set up an appointment with a doctor to see what was wrong. She had missed a fair amount of school over the years and was starting to worry that her constant exhaustion would keep her from going to the college of her choice the way her older brother had. Anna simply felt too tired to do what she wanted and needed to do.

After Anna's family practitioner considered a diagnosis of chronic fatigue syndrome, he found that the teen was having difficulty falling asleep and getting up in the morning. So he coached her to go to bed earlier, but she simply couldn't fall asleep at the prescribed time. When he referred her to my sleep center, I took a careful history and then asked Anna to keep a sleep log, which confirmed a severe sleep phase delay and major sleep deprivation. A combination of education, light visor use, regulation of her wake-up time, and taking melatonin—plus Anna's strong motivation to make a change—reduced her exhaustion and made her feel much better in only two weeks.

One more interesting fact to add to your understanding of this problem: In a study of rats designed to measure energy expenditure, those rats that were sleep deprived nearly doubled the normal expenditure, creating a huge drain on the body. In metabolic mapping of brain structures, increased energy consumption in the body has been associated with diminished brain function.

Digestion

Remember the patient I mentioned earlier in the chapter who said that lack of sleep caused his digestive tract to become inflamed? Unfortunately that teen learned the hard way that, when it comes to sleep deprivation, there is a mind-body connection; loss of sleep is considered to be a source of psychophysiological, or mind-body, stress.

I've already talked about the fact that sleep loss can contribute not only to emotional, behavioral, and learning issues but to physical problems such as headaches and more frequent infections. Now there is proof that lack of sleep can also cause stomach distress, a problem a number of my patients have suffered with. A study of partial sleep deprivation in rats showed that 30 to 50 percent of the animals developed visible stomach ulcers—which means the lining of their stomachs was actually damaged—within just 7 to 14 days. Researchers concluded that the cause of the ulcers was partial sleep deprivation, which compromised the integrity of the stomach wall by increasing the secretion of gastric acid, reducing blood flow to the stomach and changing blood adrenaline levels.

Too much caffeine, as many coffee and tea lovers know, also can lead to stomach upset. And since many teens gulp down a number of caffeinated drinks to help them get through their day, they can actually add to their stomach problems while trying to feel better. Stress and drinking too much alcohol also are known to cause stomachaches, and both can result in severe sleep deprivation.

Growth

When adolescents sleep, they not only refresh and repair their bodies, they also grow. During the third and fourth stages of sleep, which I'll talk about more in the next chapter, a growth hormone called somatotropin is secreted. In addition to having several other functions, this growth hormone stimulates the secretion of another hormone called IGF-I, which in turn stimulates both bone and muscle growth.

A number of studies have tried to determine whether growing children who are sleep deprived grow less well than those who get adequate rest. One, published in 2000, showed that when normal growth hormone secretion is blunted at night it is compensated for the next day, thereby arguing against the belief that sleep problems can inhibit growth in children. But another study in 2004 revealed that partial sleep deprivation nearly abolished pulses of growth hormone and suppressed concentrations of growth hormone, arguing that sleep deprivation does inhibit growth. Even if greatly reduced secretion of growth hormones is made up for the next day, however, we don't know if we get the same result from it—if you're up and around and doing all the things you need to do during the day, is growth hormone secretion able to produce the same results as it does when you're at rest? Clearly more research is needed, but it might be that sleep deprivation can prevent teens from growing as fully as they should.

Acne and Other Skin Problems

Ah, pimples: the bane of teenagers' existence. Nearly every adolescent experiences a breakout at some point, with girls suffering the most eruptions between 14 and 17 and boys between 16 and 19. Dirt, microbes, and several other culprits can be the cause of the apperance of pimples, but severe acne breakouts have also been reported after prolonged sleep deprivation.

Ted Grossbart, a psychologist on the faculty of Harvard Medical

School and author of the book *Skin Deep*, studies the mind-body connection in skin diseases. Grossbart points out that emotional issues can trigger outbreaks or make existing outbreaks worse, but he has also found that sleep disturbances sometimes result in higher levels of hormones and adrenaline, which can increase production of the oily substance sebum that clogs pores. Paul Martin, in his book *Counting Sheep: The Science and Pleasures of Sleep and Dreams*, notes that sleep deprivation weakens the skin's ability to act as a barrier against dirt. He also points to a study in which animals that were deprived of sleep for long periods developed what he called "unsightly skin disorders." The National Sleep Foundation states that sleep deprivation makes one more prone to pimples and contributes to acne and other skin problems. While more research is ongoing, it looks as though lack of sleep, especially for adolescents and young adults, can increase and worsen skin problems.

Kids who get their "beauty rest," though, can significantly improve their skin's appearance. Recently, when I went to greet a patient in my waiting room, I looked and looked and couldn't find him. But he was sitting there—I just didn't recognize him. He'd finally been getting the sleep he needed, and his acne had cleared up considerably and his sallow skin had pinked up. Not only that, but being rested had also erased that baggy-eyed, bedraggled look he had sported for so long. And because he wasn't as irritable and angry as he had been, he looked a lot better—and readily acknowledged he was a lot happier.

Pain

According to research studies, sleep deprivation, especially the restriction of REM sleep time, may cause increased sensitivity to acute pain. The Arthritis Foundation of New South Wales reports that sleep loss can precipitate muscle pain and that it's likely that at least some of the pain that accompanies arthritis and other joint disorders is associated with sleep deprivation. Sleep loss interferes with the body's ability to heal and can aggravate pain and discomfort. Medically healthy kids whose sleep is restricted may also take longer to recover from bumps, bruises, and broken bones.

Caffeine and Alcohol

It makes perfect sense: Tired teens who need to stay awake through a full day of classes, activities, sports, and socializing are going to do what they need to do to feel more alert and alive. And for many teens, instead of napping, exercising, or eating better for greater energy, that often means turning to caffeinated drinks. Like exhausted adults who need their morning jolt of java to even think about starting the day, more and more sleep-deprived teens are consuming caffeine—the 2006 Sleep in America poll reports that more than three-quarters of adolescents drink caffeinated beverages during the day. A number of my young patients tell me they drink five or six cups of coffee a day on an ongoing basis.

Caffeine, like other stimulants, provides users with a brief burst of energy and sense of well-being. But if you keep drinking it throughout the day to keep that feel-awake feeling going, it can wind up keeping you awake and alert well into the night. If you have to get up at the usual time the next day, you sleep even less and wake up feeling more tired—and turn to caffeine again.

To make matters worse, consuming caffeine can also decrease the quality of the little sleep you get. In a study published in the journal *Pediatrics*, 191 seventh- through ninth-graders reported their daily caffeine intake and the amount of sleep they got over a two-week period. Higher caffeine intake—up to 800 milligrams per day, the equivalent of eight cups of coffee—was associated with shorter nighttime sleep, increased wake time after sleep began, and increased daytime sleep. The study also documented increased sleep fragmentation and trouble staying asleep once the kids finally dozed off.

Are you rethinking your own four daily cups of coffee? And starting to wonder about banning soft drinks and other caffeine carriers from the fridge? Here's one other fact to add to your thinking: A recent study correlated caffeine intake with mood deterioration—which means your teen's mood, and your own, may go downhill even further when you use caffeine to try to pump up your energy after a short or bad night's sleep.

Caffeine is addictive. If you drink it long enough, you become dependent on it for stimulation. And if you finally decide there are

COUNT YOUR CAFFEINE

The following table identifies the number of milligrams of caffeine found in soda, coffee, tea, ice cream, chocolate, and some over-the-counter medications.

	Caffeine Content (mg)
Beverages	
Aqua Blast—1/2 liter	90
Barq's Root Beer—12 oz.	22
Coca-Cola Classic, Diet Coke—12 oz.	46
Coffee—8 oz.	100
Dr. Pepper—12 oz.	42
Espresso—2 oz.	100
Hot chocolate—6 oz.	20
Java Water—1/2 liter	125
Juiced—10 oz.	60
Krank—1/2 liter	100
Mountain Dew—12 oz.	55
Pepsi, Diet Pepsi—12 oz.	37
Red Bull—8 oz.	80
7 Up—12 oz.	0
Snapple Iced Tea—16 oz.	55
Sunkist orange soda—12 oz.	42
Tea, black—8 oz.	50
Tea, green—8 oz.	30
Foods	
Ben & Jerry's non-fat coffee yogurt—1 cup	85
Dark chocolate—2 oz.	50
Haagen-Dazs coffee ice cream—I cup	58
Hershey bar—1.5 oz.	10
Milk chocolate—2 oz.	30
Starbucks coffee ice cream—1 cup	40–60
Over-the-Counter Medication	
Anacin—2 tablets	64
Excedrin—2 tablets	130
NoDoz Regular Strength—1 tablet	100
NoDoz Maxi Strength—1 tablet	200
Vivarin—1 tablet	200

better ways to feel more alert, quitting the stuff can leave you with days of severe headaches and possibly the jitters from withdrawal. (Cutting back slowly, by half a cup a day, can help lessen those effects.)

In addition to increased caffeine use, sleep deprivation can also result in increased use of alcohol, nicotine, and other dangerous substances. Teens who are too tired to exercise, stressed from arguments with parents or friends, worried about keeping up in class, or just generally feeling down about how they look or feel may turn to alcohol or other drugs to cope or to ease the pain. On their own, all of these substances are, of course, addictive and bad for your health and safety. But using them when you're sleepy heightens their effect. Studies show that impairments that result from combining drugs with sleep deprivation are greater than those that result from each alone.

SNOOZE NEWS

According to the National Sleep Foundation's 2005 Sleep in America poll, adults who drink four or more caffeinated beverages a day sleep less, have more daytime sleepiness, and take longer to fall asleep.

Interpersonal Relationships

If you've read through most of this chapter, you probably won't be surprised that a sleep-deprived teen might have some problems with interpersonal relationships. Most likely you've seen that effect for yourself, not only in your own relationship with your child but in her relationships with friends and other family members. Just being an adolescent can make developing and sustaining relationships difficult; adolescents' strong emotions and volatility can cause ruptures with friends and arguments with family. But an exhausted teen has even fewer resources for staying on an even keel with pals and loved ones.

Sleep-deprived teens have less patience to see things through. So if they have words with a friend, they might not be able to wait until the blowup simmers down. Being irritable and edgy can provoke them to act immediately and unreasonably—and perhaps cause them to lose a friend.

Being constantly tired can also cause teens to miss school and activities. Along with losing class and learning time and perhaps exercise or honing a skill, that means they also miss out on time with their friends. Particularly during the teen years, friendships can go up and down, and not sharing experiences with friends can loosen the ties that bind.

In the home, exhaustion can of course cause strain as well. Sleep-deprived teens are going to be grouchy, quick to take offense, forget or be slow to help with chores, and not have the energy for family outings or other fun. There's so much potential for clashing, in fact, that parent-child relationships can be stretched until they snap.

Stress and the Ability to Cope

Sleep deprivation's effects can make your teenager pretty miserable—less healthy, less happy, and less able to perform well. And all of that can add up to one giant case of stress. Though society is telling them that they need to do it all, teens' exhausted minds and bodies are simply not up to the job. That can make many teenagers extremely anxious and distressed, to the point where they not only don't know what to do but shut down completely. A number of kids who have come to my sleep lab are so stressed out that they're barely capable of functioning.

All of those kids are in need of more and better sleep. It's the ticket not only to reducing stress but to managing the other negative conditions described in this chapter. (Getting enough sleep yourself will help you lower your own stress level and maintain better health as well as set that all-important good example for your teen.) But what is sleep really? And how does it help us live more productive and successful lives? In the next chapter I discuss what happens when we sleep and help you to understand all the forces that are at play.

LESS SLEEP CAN EQUAL MORE STRESS

In an experiment that monitored students the week they were evaluated for acceptance to a graduate program, those who scored high on the stress scale reported significantly reduced total sleep times.

3

Inside Sleep: What It Is, How It Works, Why Teens Need It

In the first two chapters, I talked about the many problems that teens who don't get enough sleep can have: Not only can they stay awake way into the night and drive *you* to distraction, but they can suffer numerous negative effects on their health, performance, relationships, and well-being. In this chapter I focus on all the good things sleep does and why an adequate amount is necessary for top functioning and quality of life. I also tell you, in the simplest of terms, exactly what goes on during sleep and why every stage is important. Don't worry, there won't be a quiz at the end, but the more you understand about sleep, the better you'll be able to help your teen understand why she should be getting more ZZZZs.

Let's start by defining sleep. Shakespeare called it the "chief nourisher in life's feast" and wrote that it "knits up the raveled sleave of care." The poet John Keats invoked it as "magic sleep" and thought of it like a nesting bird "brooding o'er the troubled sea of the mind till it is hushed and smooth." The National Sleep Foundation describes sleep as the "key to health, performance, safety, and quality of life." It's also the opposite of wakefulness, which is an alert, connected, interactive state of being in which we have control over our movement and thinking. Sleep is a complex process that is all of these things and more.

I define sleep as a multifaceted process that happens every 24 hours and that should last seven to nine hours in adults and as long as nine and a half hours in adolescents. During sleep, consciousness is significantly reduced, we disconnect from our surroundings, and our bodies engage in restorative functions—making proteins, hormones, and neurotransmitters—that enable growth, learning, and mood stabilization. Basically, sleep affects every aspect of functioning. It heals the previous day's stresses and strains—perhaps a pulled muscle or a cold—and gives us the mental and physical energy we need to function the next day—without being too grouchy. Sleep lets us—more likely, our teens!—run the 50-yard dash in the state track competition and allows us to think clearly and learn figures and facts. Adequate nighttime rest takes a body and mind that are worn out from their day and brings both back to a clean baseline.

Although sleep is a time during which we look quiet, there's actually a great deal of metabolic, or physical and chemical, activity taking place. Much of that activity takes place in the brain. Years ago scientists believed that, because the body looked quiet, the brain was quiet too and was resting like the body. But with the invention of the electro-encephalograph, which uses small metal cups glued to the scalp to record microvolts of brain wave, or EEG, activity, scientists learned that the brain, as well as the body, is hard at work while we sleep.

Sleep is critical to helping both the mind and the body maintain physical and psychological well-being. But more than 50 million Americans as well as millions of people around the world report difficulty sleeping. That means that many of us, including teens, are not living as well as we could.

How much sleep do we need to fuel our potential? I've already said that the ideal amount of sleep for adolescents is eight and a half to nine and a half hours. But it's not much less for adults: seven to nine hours (in my practice I call seven hours the lowest legal limit of sleep). And babies and small children need tons of it. But needing it and getting it are two very different things.

The 24/7 society we live in, overloaded with electronic tools and all forms of entertainment, is a major reason we don't get the sleep we

SLEEP NEEDS THROUGHOUT LIFE

The National Sleep Foundation recommends the following amounts of sleep for infants, children, teens, and adults.

Age Group	Hours
Newborns	
0–2 months	10.5–18
2–12 months	14–15
Children	
12–18 months	13–15
18 months–2 years	12–14
3–5 years	11–13
Adolescents	8.5–9.5
Adults	7–9

need (for more on the many cultural factors that promote sleep deprivation in teens, see Chapter 5). Even when we do drag ourselves away from our computers, TVs, and iPods, we often sabotage ourselves with worries and stress that interrupt and/or shorten our nights. Sleep—as it's meant to be—is a dynamic process composed of five separate stages, each of which is physiologically different and fulfills different body and brain requirements. We need to cycle through all the stages in an orderly sequence during the night and spend adequate time in each, with as few interruptions as possible, in order to reap their full benefits.

SNOOZE NEWS

Animals, like people, have different sleep requirements. Giraffes sleep only two hours a night, whereas bats sleep 20. Cats are one of the few animals that don't group most of their sleep time into one long nighttime session, preferring to sleep for fairly even chunks of time throughout the day–cat naps!

The Stages of Sleep

As I discussed in Chapter 1, sleep-wake homeostasis and the circadian rhythm drive the need for and the timing of sleep. When the hormone melatonin is first secreted in the late afternoon, it signals the brain to begin the process that leads to sleep hours later.

**HOW DOES YOUR BRAIN KNOW
WHEN TO TURN SLEEP ON?**

Falling asleep depends on several key factors:

- How many hours you've been awake (Process S)
- The influence of the day-night cycle (Process C)
- The timing of melatonin secretion
- Genetics—whether you were born a night owl or a lark
- Your behavior and the habit you get into

Stage 1

I like to call Stage 1 "boring lecture sleep" because it's the state most of us are in when we're a bit tired and sitting through a boring lecture: Our eyes close and we hear the speaker droning on only in the distant background. Stage 1 is actually a transitional stage of sleep in which you begin to disconnect from your surroundings and start moving into a nonwakeful state. While you may still feel attached to your environment—you know you're sitting in a lecture hall listening to a boring speaker—you also may experience a sense of sleepiness or fading.

Stage 1 sleep generally lasts about 10 minutes, and you can be awakened from such sleep fairly easily—often accompanied by that embarrassing full-body, falling-off-the-cliff jerk. Many people who wake up from Stage 1 will deny that they were really sleeping, even when you've been watching them twitch and snort and breathe more slowly.

Brain waves in Stage 1 are characterized by a gradual waning of the 8- to 12-cycles-per-second alpha wave rhythm that is the hallmark of relaxed wakefulness and an increase in slower, four- to seven-per-second theta wave forms that indicate sleep. Slow, horizontal roving-eye movements may be seen during this stage of sleep, and there may also be a regularization of breathing and a slight relaxation of the muscles. During the transition to Stage 1 from wakefulness, some people experience visual misperceptions called hypnogogic, or drowsiness-related, hallucinations. Others experience what they describe as a feeling of falling.

Stage 2

In Stage 2 there is a further increase in slower, relatively low-voltage, mixed-frequency theta wave activity. There are also two sleep phenomena: sleep spindles, which are runs of highly rhythmical activity predominantly in the central regions of the head that last from one-half to one and one-half seconds; and K complexes, which are distinctive high-voltage complex wave forms that are thought to be a protective response to arousal and that promote the transition to deeper stages of sleep.

While the exact purpose of Stage 2 sleep is unknown, it seems to be a stage that prepares the body to head into deeper sleep, though you definitely feel you've been asleep if you're awakened from this stage. Stage 2 accounts for 45 to 55 percent of our night's sleep.

Stages 3 and 4

In Stage 3 and Stage 4 sleep, or slow wave sleep (SWS), brain activity slows dramatically and the mixed-frequency theta activity of Stages 1 and 2 is replaced by one- to three-per-second slow waves. The distinction between Stages 3 and 4 is only in degree: When more than 20 percent of any 30-second period of sleep is composed of high-voltage slow waves, it is called Stage 3. The period is considered Stage 4 if more than 50 percent of it is composed of these waves.

In Stages 3 and 4, sleep spindles are less prominent and K complexes drop out. During both stages, breathing is deep and regular, muscles relax, blood pressure drops, and eye movement generally stops. Both stages are also a very deep period of sleep from which it's difficult to be awakened; you may have tried to wake your teen as a child and gotten scared because she seemed unconscious. Dreaming can occur during slow wave sleep, although most dreaming takes place during the fifth stage of sleep.

SWS constitutes about 20 percent of your night's sleep. During this period, growth hormone is secreted, muscles rest and receive an increased supply of blood, the immune system is active, and tissue growth and repair take place. Energy is restored and, if we get enough SWS, we wake feeling great and physically ready to face the day. But if we don't, we can feel not just tired but achy and disoriented.

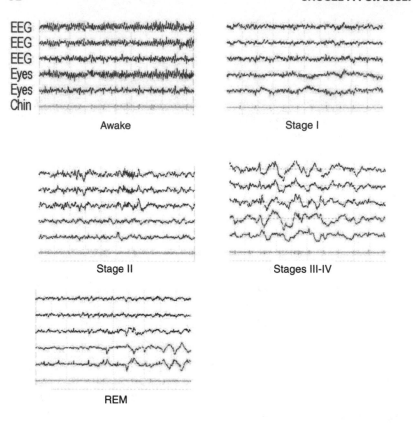

The five stages of the sleep-wake cycle are distinct with different patterns of brain wave activity (EEG), eye movements, and muscle tone (chin).

In Stage 4 SWS, the arousal threshold is very high. But if you're awakened abruptly, you may experience "parasomnias" such as sleep walking, sleep talking, or night terrors (episodes of screaming and agitation during the first half of the night). All of these phenomena occur between sleep and wakefulness—you aren't fully awake but you also aren't fully asleep, and you usually transition back to sleep without waking up. Parasomnias are considered to be normal occurrences and happen more frequently in childhood and adolescence than in adulthood.

Stage 5

This stage of sleep wasn't clearly described and understood until the early 1950s. It's a very different type of sleep from the other four because in those stages there's little or no eye movement; Stage 5 features bursts of rapid side-to-side eye movement under our eyelids. That darting movement gives the stage its name: REM, or rapid eye movement, sleep. The first four stages of sleep are often referred to together as NREM, or non-rapid eye movement, sleep.

SLEEP-RELATED DISCOVERIES

With the invention of the electroencephalogram and the discovery of all five stages of sleep, sleep researcher J. Allan Hobson noted that "more has been learned about sleep in the past 60 years than in the preceding 6,000." Yet there is still much to learn and understand today.

REM sleep accounts for nearly one-quarter of our total sleep time. We cycle into it approximately every 90 minutes but the first episodes are short and those later in the night are much longer. In REM sleep, as in SWS, it's very hard to wake up. It's also a time of intense dreaming, and the dreams may have strange spatial relationships, colors, and ideas. Bizarre emotions may surface in frightening dreams, but the majority of REM-related dreams are usually pleasant.

It is during REM sleep that the psyche is restored, and recent evidence shows that REM sleep is also involved in the processing of information (see Chapter 4 for more on the sleep-learning link). During REM sleep we breathe faster, our heartbeat is more irregular, and speeded-up brain wave activity makes it look like we're awake.

A key feature of REM sleep is that, except for the bursts of rapid eye movement and synchronous activity in the inner ear, no other parts of our bodies can move—our muscles are paralyzed. If you've ever had a dream in which you tried to run away from the bogeyman or wanted to speak or scream but couldn't, you were having a REM dream and the paralysis of your body was incorporated into your dream.

Why can't you move during REM sleep? We believe the paralysis of REM sleep is a protective reflex. During this sleep, we're not conscious of the outside world, and current theories suggest that our brains are rehashing all the information received during the day, as well as analyzing memories and forming brand new ones. During this work, frightening or dangerous thoughts can occur, and the paralysis of our muscles prevents us from acting on those thoughts and dreams.

People with a condition called REM Sleep Behavioral Disorder, which interferes with REM paralysis, can respond to a dream with dangerous movement. For example, if they're having a dream in which someone is chasing them, they can jump out of bed and start running away—and crash into a bedside table or fall. If they're dreaming that they're in a fight with someone, they can punch or kick the person sleeping next to them. If we were able to move during REM sleep and act on our dreams, we could end up in the hospital—or always have to sleep alone.

SNOOZE NEWS

Because REM sleep combines a very active brain with a paralyzed body, it is sometimes called paradoxical sleep.

REM sleep appears to be particularly important to the developing child and adolescent. Studies on the effects of sleep deprivation suggest that REM sleep deprivation in newborns can negatively affect central nervous system development, and permanent sleep disruption early in life can cause an abnormal number of neural cells to die. REM sleep is also crucial for the anabolic, or energy building and healing, activities that take place in the brain and in the body.

The Cycles of Sleep

Once you've snoozed your way from boring-lecture sleep through REM sleep, you're said to have completed one cycle of sleep. A full cycle takes approximately 90 to 120 minutes, so if you get all the rest you need, you'll go through four or five cycles each night.

But on the second through the fourth or fifth cycles, things change a bit. After you complete REM sleep, you may only briefly pass through boring-lecture sleep or skip it entirely before moving into Stage 2 and then completing the stages through Stage 5 again. The time you spend in each stage also changes; the first half of the night is spent mostly in

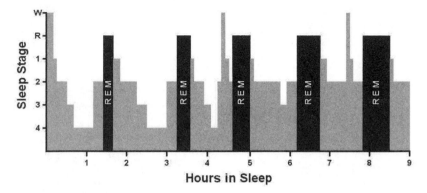

Sleep hypnogram illustrating how the average teen cycles through the five stages of sleep during the course of the night.

SWS and the second half mostly in REM sleep. By sleeping uninterrupted through all of the stages, while in tune with the day-night cycle, you give your body and mind the time they need to heal the previous day's wear and tear and reenergize for the day ahead.

The Times They Are A-Changin'

Although it's clear that people of all ages need to get regular, adequate amounts of sleep if they want to function at their best, today's homo sapiens sleep much less than their predecessors did and their sleep patterns are often irregular and interrupted. In the agrarian society of our not-too-distant past, sleep was much easier to come by. There was no electricity, so there was no TV to watch, no telephone to gab on, no computer for playing games, no CDs to listen to. In the evenings families could, of course, sit around the piano and sing or read or talk by candlelight, but most of today's distractions weren't available then, which made going to bed not long after dark much more likely.

And, of course there were the cows—which made getting up at a reasonable time also more likely. Milking, feeding animals, and starting to work in the fields before the extreme heat of midday made waking and rising with the sun not just natural but a necessity. Most people were entrained to the day-night cycle, and most found that the hard physical labor that filled their days caused them to sleep an average of

The times they are a–changin'

but can evolution keep up?

Limited activities and distractions along with a more physically active lifestyle allowed more time for sleep in 1905 compared to 2005.

10 hours a night, healing their bodies and getting them ready for the next challenging day.

Today, of course, we sleep much less. As the chart on page 49 shows, seven to nine hours of sleep is considered adequate for adults, and many of us don't get anywhere near that amount. The same definitely goes for teens. On average, we're sleeping an hour and a half less a night than we did at the beginning of the 20th century, a truly shocking reduction. Yet at the same time that we're sleeping much less, we're asking much more of our bodies and minds.

Today people are making demands on themselves as they never have before. If you think about how humans and animals have evolved, you'll remember that it takes centuries for new capabilities to develop. But the digital age has pushed us to become more capable more quickly, and with that intense push has come a huge increase in the demand for alertness. We need to stay awake and functioning if we're going to survive in our constantly connected, constantly advancing culture. Just think of all the devices that you—and your teen—live with every minute of the day—as well as during the night. Is that a pager I see on your belt? Is there a cell phone in your bag? When did you last check your e-mail? Is that a fax I hear coming in from across the ocean—at 3:30 a.m. your time?

The need to "stay in the game" has pushed us to expect much more from our bodies. But we are expecting those bodies to keep up on less sleep and therefore less time for repair and renewal—which makes us unable to evolve in tandem with our environment.

That may spell disaster not just for us but for our children, because one of the ways humans evolve is through natural selection—the process through which the organisms that are best suited to their environment survive and pass their genetic material on to the next generation. By raising sleep-deprived teens, we may be putting them at greater risk for long-term disease complications; we know that sleep deprivation weakens the immune system. But until more studies are done, we won't know if sleep deprivation during the teen years has more far-reaching implications on adult health and longevity.

We do know that teens today, just like adults, are much more sleep deprived than they used to be. A study by Roseanne Armitage reported that 24 percent of college students in 1978 complained of being constantly tired; in 2002 that number exploded to 71 percent. We also know that negative impacts result not just from sleepiness but from sustained wakefulness—our bodies just can't operate at full tilt when we push ourselves to stay awake for more than 15 or 16 hours.

Teens, of course, are in touch with their friends, as well as the rest of the universe, for more than 16 hours a day. My latest reminder of that fact came on a recent trip with my daughter Elyssa to tour several colleges. After getting completely lost looking for our motel the first night, I staggered into bed in our shared room and she eventually followed. But at 1:00 a.m. her cell phone rang—and she answered it! After talking to her friend for a few minutes, she headed back to sleep, and I tried to do the same. But at 2:30 the phone rang again! This time Elyssa slept right through the ring—but I bet you can guess who didn't.

Our 24/7 society is wreaking havoc with our natural rhythms and needs. While we still have the reflex that makes us feel sleepy, we don't still have the reflex that makes us stop what we're doing and go to sleep—we've found untold ways to override it. Over the years we've stretched and stretched our daytime alert hours until, for many of us, including our teens, night and day have become pretty much the same.

As we become more and more sleep deprived, "state instability" develops: Our state of wakefulness destabilizes, we can't remain alert, and there's a blurring of the boundaries between wakefulness and sleep. When that happens we're subject to:

• Microsleeps—very brief stretches of sleep interrupting our consciousness; microsleeps cause us to miss hearing bits of information
• Sleep attacks—periods of sleep that occur inadvertently and often without warning
• Lapses in cognition—periods of mental fogginess during which we have timeouts in function that can last up to 18 seconds

The Gene Factor

Don't most kids love to blame things on their parents? Well, here's their chance to do it again—but this time with some cause. Unfortunately, for long-suffering parents everywhere, having trouble falling asleep before midnight might not be due only to pubertal, environmental, or cultural factors. It might also be something that teens can actually hold their parents accountable for.

Clearly some adults find it easier to stay up later than others. These night owls are alert and energized far later in the evening than most of us, and they have a good deal of difficulty getting up in the morning for work or school. Though they're past the age when their brains are wired to cause this late-to-bed, late-to-rise syndrome, their natural body rhythm is to go to sleep later and wake up later—they still have a sleep phase delay. Often adult night owls are tired all morning and afternoon and then begin to come into their own as everyone else is winding down.

Now here's the blame part. Just the way brown eyes, full cheeks, and the ability (or inability) to understand math can be passed from mother or father to son or daughter, the tendency to be a "night person" can be handed down to children; if a parent is a night owl, there's a significant chance that her child will be one too. DR1 markers, one group of human leukocyte antigens, which are markers in the white blood cells that help identify a variety of conditions, including whether or not a person is a good bone marrow donor, were positive in a statistically significant number of people who were sleep phase delayed. That suggested to the researchers conducting the study that there is a genetic predisposition to Delayed Sleep Phase Syndrome.

Often when young patients come in to see me because they can't fall asleep before 1:00 or 2:00 in the morning, it turns out that one or both parents have the same problem. These adults may have found a way to live with the situation, perhaps by working in a job that doesn't require an early start or by running their own business and setting their own hours, but their teens generally are not as lucky; they don't have the lifestyle choices that adults do.

A friend of mine, for example, really wanted to have a third child but knew from her experiences waking up to nurse her first two children several times a night that she couldn't tolerate months and months of interrupted sleep and sleep deprivation again—it made her completely incapable of functioning, both at home and at work. So she made the choice to have another baby, but to provide a college student with room and board in exchange for getting up in the night to give the baby her bottles. My friend knew her limits and had the freedom and the wherewithal to come up with a workable solution for her problem.

When a teen night owl comes to see me and we determine that she is from a night-owl family, I generally am more aggressive and try to

A TEEN'S TAKE

"My dad is definitely not a night owl. He falls asleep five minutes after he turns on the TV or lies down. My mom, though, is a different story. She doesn't go to sleep until after I do, and I'm up till at least 11:00. Then it takes me some time to fall asleep."

engage the entire household in the treatment plan. That's because it's particularly tough to change a teenager's wake-up time if no one else in the family is getting up in the morning and the household culture is to stay up late. It's definitely harder to change a teen's sleep pattern when not only puberty is involved but genetics as well. This double whammy can take time to turn around. (If you or your spouse is a night owl, see Chapter 12 for ideas on how you can set a good sleep model for your teen.)

To add to the bank of potentially inheritable sleep problems, cutting-edge studies have shown that there may be a genetic link to the length of time a person sleeps. If one parent is a "short sleeper"—he or she naturally goes to sleep late and wakes up early—the child will be predisposed to be a short sleeper too.

An Important Period for Sleep

While getting enough high-quality sleep at any age is crucial, it's particularly important for adolescents. Not only do they need it for all the growing and changing and learning they must accomplish, and to function at their best, but they need to establish a healthy sleep habit for all the years ahead. Teens who stay up well into the night and are exhausted all day can let an age-related problem turn into a life-long pattern of living. As teens make the transition from child to adult, they can add greatly to their chances of enjoying a healthy future if they start following a healthy sleep pattern.

SLEEP FOR TEENS IQ TEST

Ask your teen to take this National Sleep Foundation quiz to check her understanding of what happens during sleep and why she needs more sleep than she's getting. It's a good idea for you and the rest of your family to take the test too.

1. During sleep, your brain rests. (T or F)
2. You can learn to function normally with two or three hours less sleep than your body actually needs per night. (T or F)
3. Teens go to sleep and wake later because they are lazy. (T or F)
4. Although you may not get enough sleep during the week, you can catch up on your sleep on weekends and still have healthy sleep habits. (T or F)
5. Boredom makes you feel sleepy, even if you have had enough sleep. (T or F)
6. Resting in bed with your eyes closed cannot satisfy your body's need for sleep. (T or F)
7. Snoring is not harmful as long as it does not disturb others or wake you up.* (T or F)
8. Most people do not know when they are sleepy. (T or F)
9. Turning up the radio, opening the window, or turning on the air conditioner will help you stay awake while driving. (T or F)
10. Sleep disorders are mainly due to worry or psychological problems. (T or F)
11. Everyone dreams every night. (T or F)
12. Driving after being awake for 18 hours puts you at the same level of risk for a crash as someone who is legally drunk. (T or F)

Answers: 1. F, 2. F, 3. F, 4. F, 5. F, 6. T, 7. F, 8. T, 9. F, 10. F, 11. T, 12. T

* Snoring may be a sign of sleep apnea; see Chapter 7 for details.

4

The Sleep-Learning Link:
Why All-Nighters Don't Work

Have you ever used the expression "I'll sleep on it"? Often, when we have a big decision to make or need to figure out how to do something, we give ourselves more time to think by waiting until the next day to give our answer. But waiting until the next day doesn't just let us put off making a decision. Sleeping on the issue also gives us the time we need to learn about and understand it so that the answer becomes clear.

Just as a good night's sleep helps us fight infection, stabilize our mood, lower our stress, and look better, according to recent research it also lets us organize, process, and understand the information we took in during the day—in other words, learn. While we've known that sleep repairs and refreshes the body, we now know that it also has a significantly positive effect on learning and memory.

This evidence, which has been well documented only since the beginning of this century, has enormous importance for everyone but especially adolescents, because they spend a huge portion of their waking hours involved in some kind of learning, from chemistry to a second language to perfecting their soccer skills to driving a car. We used to think that that kind of learning took place only while you sat with your nose in a textbook or on the soccer field or while a parent sat beside you gripping the door handle while you stalled the car in the middle of the intersection. But now it's clear that during the night we consolidate the information we took in during the day and make it our own.

Uncovering this fact has put sleep deprivation in a whole new light. Not only does it cause us to function at a much lower level, it also causes us to learn at a much lower level. For teens that can mean not only getting C's instead of A's but forgetting how to execute a football play, play a classical piano piece, recreate the perfect sunset on canvas, or do complex math problems on the SAT. According to a report by the American Academy of Pediatrics, it can also mean that students are less motivated to do their best at school and less receptive to teaching. As one teen said, "I miss out on a lot of details because I lose focus and the ability to concentrate when I'm severely sleep deprived. I'm also quite forgetful when I'm tired."

Just how does sleep deprivation prevent us from learning well? To understand that, you need to understand what's involved in learning and how the brain takes in information and makes it available to us when we need it. Let's take a look at that now. (One note here: When I talk about learning, I'm going to use the terms "memory" and "learning" interchangeably, because they're so closely linked that they're really the same thing. When you remember something, you have learned it.)

How We Learn

The first thing to understand is that the brain is not like a computer memory chip on which information is stored. The brain is plastic, which means it constantly changes and adapts to the data it acquires. When we acquire information during the day that we want to save as a memory—the fact that Eleanor Roosevelt helped found UNICEF or that to open the front door we have to turn the deadbolt key to the left—the information goes into a particular region of the brain, called the hippocampus. But that region is only a holding zone, and the information is actually in jeopardy there, because before the brain can process and consolidate it, it might get involved in other activities. Say, for example, you call Information for a phone number, but before you can dial it your friend calls and you spend five minutes on the phone hearing all about a workshop she wants you to go to with her. When you hang up and start to dial the number you just got, you can't remember it—much to your annoyance—and have to call Information again. There wasn't time for the phone number to become installed in your holding zone.

It's during the night, when you're sleeping, that multiple neuronal pathways are laid down to take the information in the holding zone to the appropriate regions of the brain for consolidating and refining. In other words, it's during sleep when memories become a permanent part of your brain, letting you call them up at any time.

MEMORIES AREN'T JUST FACTS

Researchers have grouped memories into two different categories—declarative and nondeclarative, or procedural. Declarative memories are based on facts: what you did yesterday, your brother-in-law's birthday, the fact that the freezing point of water is 32 degrees Fahrenheit. Nondeclarative memories have to do with procedures, actions, and skills—for example, how to play a chord on the guitar or build a picnic table. There are also several types of memories: sensory, motor, visual, and auditory.

But the process of learning doesn't stop there. Over time, memories continue to be adjusted and elaborated at the molecular, cellular, and system levels. Once made permanent, memories are constantly refined.

Why does that happen after the precious nuggets have been safely stored? Basically, so that they become more efficient and accessible, so that you don't have to struggle to remember how to do something or take forever to remember the answer to a question. As it reorganizes and polishes your memories, your brain is working to lay down a superfast highway on which you can receive the information you need on autopilot—the information just comes to you innately; you don't have to stop and think to figure it out.

That superfast highway connects several different areas of the brain. For example, if you're about to make a jump shot in a basketball game, you need to access your stored memories on how far you should raise your arms, where your feet should be, and how fast you should move to make the shot. That information comes from the parietal lobe, which gathers information related to where you are in space. If you need to know how to spell "accommodations" in a letter you're writing, the information (two c's and two m's) comes from the fronto-temporal cortex, which stores information on speech and language. When activated, the appropriate parts of the brain send the appropriate information to the cerebral cortex, which then tells your body what to do—smoothly and naturally.

And that, of course, is great for you. Because not only will you easily know the answer to a question and look like a star to your boss or your family or your teachers or your friends, you'll also be giving your brain the opportunity to work on something else—the mental energy you would have used to figure out the question at hand can be used instead for another task or put to work to learn something else. If, for example, your brain has consolidated and refined the information you need to create and bake your world-renowned chocolate mousse cake, you can make it without having to spend a second of thought on it—and help your son with his vocabulary words at the same time. Once permanently installed, smoothly functioning memories let you multitask and have plenty of brainpower available for wherever you need to apply it.

So, to sum up here, we acquire information as we go about our lives during the day, then consolidate and assimilate it as memories for permanent housing in our brain while we sleep at night, then refine and enhance those memories to make them more usable, all in a process that lets us call up memories and use them over a long period of time.

When We Learn

The second thing to understand is the time period in which we learn. As I said above, our daytime memories are consolidated and made permanent while we hit the mattress for our minimum of seven hours of rest at night. But when exactly does that learning take place? Is it all night long or only during certain stages?

For quite some time, researchers believed that learning took place only during the fifth, or REM, stage of sleep; in fact, when a task was studied that showed that REM sleep wasn't involved in its comprehension, some scientists continued to believe that sleep wasn't involved in learning at all. Now, however, not only is it certain that sleep is involved in learning, but as we continue to test tasks we're finding that every stage of sleep has an important part in making it happen.

In general, it appears that NREM, or non-REM, sleep—the first four stages of sleep—facilitates declarative, or facts-and-figures, learning. REM sleep, the last stage of the sleep cycle, seems to enable the consolidation of procedural, or more complex, learning. Enhanced sleep-dependent performance, in fact, has been associated with both slow wave sleep in the early part of the night and REM sleep in the later part of the night. Some researchers believe, though, that both types of sleep affect learning in a complementary and sequential way. Studies of birds have shown that both slow wave sleep, the kind found in Stages 3 and 4, and REM sleep play complementary roles in their memory consolidation.

But whether or not the different kinds of learning take place in one stage of sleep or across several stages, we need a full night of uninterrupted sleep, cycling through all the stages to the maximum extent, to give our brain the time it needs to lay down, consolidate, and enhance both types of memory. Only in this way can we learn much of anything—studies show that less than six hours of sleep the night following information intake blocks the positive effect of sleep on learning.

But one night of great sleep is not enough. To really cement the learning that's taking place, the brain needs three consecutive nights of adequate, regular rest. But the first night is key—if you don't get enough sleep then, the information you took in gets wiped out and isn't necessarily recoverable on the second and third nights. In your teen's case, if she starts reading a book the day before a test on it and stays up till 2:00 a.m. to finish it, all the information that was taken in won't be there come test time if the bus arrives for pickup at 7:15. In simple terms, all-nighters don't work; sleep does. As a good friend always said in college when faced with a big exam the next day, better

A College Student Says . . .

❝ *Freshman year, the night before two finals, I pulled an all-nighter. During the second final, for psychology, I actually fell asleep. Not only didn't I have enough time to finish, but I couldn't concentrate very well and I couldn't remember half of what I had studied. It was the last time I stayed up all night studying before an exam.* ❞

---

to be well rested than well read. (Of course, it's actually better to be both!)

How are we sure that we're really learning while we sleep? Probably you've witnessed it for yourself, though you may not have realized it at the time. Think back to a time when you had to make a big decision—say, whether you were ready to leave a job you really liked but were no longer challenged by. You likely gathered lots of information—what the job market was like, the names of people you could contact who might know of available positions, how comfortable you would feel changing companies or even your career at this point in your life—but you just couldn't come to grips with the question. To try to stop obsessing, you reviewed statistics and names and assessed your inner feelings and then gave yourself a deadline of the following day. Wisely, you slept on your decision—and were amazed to discover when you woke up that you knew exactly the right thing to do.

You can also see proof that you learn during the night by taking a simple finger-tapping test, the point being to see how many times you can tap your finger, or four fingers in sequence, in a certain amount of time. For example, try tapping four fingers in sequence, from pinky to index finger, at 10:00 in the morning for 30 seconds; write down how many times you complete the sequence. Then try the same thing again at 10:00 at night—the number of completions should be about the same. But then repeat the exercise the following morning—and be surprised. You'll probably see an improvement in speed of up to 26 percent—a huge gain. Studies have shown that people taking this test continue to improve over a three-night period in both speed and accuracy—without practicing at all in between.

We also have proof of sleep's effect on learning on a very scientific level. Researchers are now able to map the brain with brain imaging devices, and those scans show that patterns of regional brain activation associated with daytime learning are seen again during sleep, as though the brain were replaying, strengthening, and refining the events of the day. But following a night of sleep, studies have shown, the patterns change, indicating a refining of the memories. After several nights, once the information has been fully learned and becomes an automatic memory, the parietal lobe, which is involved in daytime information recognition, is no longer activated and is free to become involved in learning something else.

Studies have also shown that sleep can restore memories. Once information has been acquired and become a memory, it can still deteriorate during the course of a day. An experiment carried out by S. C. Mednick et al. asked a number of people to do a visual texture discrimination task several times during a day. The researchers found that performance deteriorated over the course of four tests—and that a midday nap taken between the second and third tests restored performance. Another study by K. M. Fenn et al. found that, while his subjects' recognition of novel words decreased during the day following training, their performance was restored the following morning after a night's sleep. Not only does sleep enhance the learning of information, it restores memory as well.

Taking on the Tough Stuff

From all that sleep researchers have seen and studied, we know for a fact that sleep is crucial to learning. To sum it up, a full night's sleep, covering all five stages:

- Is necessary for the consolidation of memory
- Enhances procedural learning
- Restores task performance that has deteriorated
- Improves learning without practicing the task
- Is needed in the first 24 hours after taking in the information in order to optimize learning

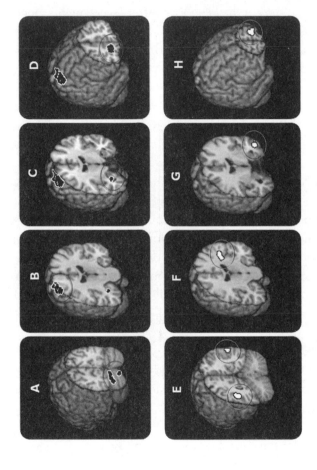

These functional brain scans (fMRI) were obtained after subjects were trained on a motor sequence task and performance was retested after a night's sleep. The blackened areas in the circles in figures A-D show areas of increased activation during the task after sleep and the white areas in E-H show areas of decreased activation. This study demonstrates that sleep-dependent motor learning is associated with large-scale plastic reorganization of memory throughout several brain regions, allowing skilled motor movements to be executed more quickly, more accurately, and more automatically following sleep.

Reproduced with permission of Matthew Walker, Ph.D., Sleep and Neuroimaging Laboratory, Harvard Medical School, Boston, MA.

A High School Swimmer Says . . .

" *Last year, whenever I had a swim meet, I was really disappointed in my performance. Even though I was getting up at 5:00 every morning to get in a good practice before school started, I just wasn't doing any better. It took me a while to figure it out—well, actually my coach figured it out. On the nights before meets, and, really, most of the other nights, I was only getting around five hours' sleep. Once I started clocking closer to seven hours I started doing a lot better.* **"**

However, sleep is most effective for learning things that are difficult. And that's true for all kinds of learning, including motor related, auditory, visual, and behavioral.

Motor-Based Learning

Sleep is critical to developing the skills needed for playing sports and doing other high-level physical activities. It's not enough for teens to practice the particular motor skills they need after school during practice; to make them their own, to truly learn them, they have to lay down the necessary neuronal pathways that will enable them to perform the actions innately and seamlessly. To learn complex motor skills and sequences, perhaps a complex springboard dive or a lengthy cheerleading routine, they need to get adequate, regular, and uninterrupted sleep.

> **SNOOZE NEWS**
>
> REM sleep has been found to be involved in the reprocessing and optimization of high-order information. Restricting REM sleep interferes with complex associative learning.

A study of sleep-dependent motor sequences pointed up sleep's effectiveness for learning difficult steps. You can see the proof of this yourself, though, if you practice a five-step motor sequence you want to learn, perhaps a new dance step. After you practice the sequence, you won't see much improvement after a night's sleep, because that number of moves is something you can pick up fairly easily. But if you try to learn a nine-step sequence, maybe several intricate dance steps in combination, you'll see a huge improvement the next day following a good night's sleep.

The length of time you're awake between when you learn a skill and when you sleep doesn't make any difference to the learning—it's the sleep that does it. A study reported in *Clinical Sports Medicine* also reported that spending more time learning the skill didn't change the effect of sleeping—the acquisition of the skill and the enhancement of the memory during sleep appeared to involve two different brain mechanisms. But as with making any memory your own, the first night's sleep after learning a motor sequence is critical for consolidating it—and adding two more nights of great sleep leads to overall enhancement, especially for more complex skills; it also enables the action to become automatic without further training. Even if a diver or dancer follows up a sleep-deprived first night after training with a solid night of sleep, though, the enhanced learning ordinarily provided by sleep the first night after a task is learned is blocked and can't be recovered with future nights' sleep.

SNOOZE NEWS Researchers have confirmed the relationship between sleep and learning, but some have linked motor learning to the amount of time spent in REM sleep and others to the time spent in slow wave, or non-REM, sleep. However, all found that motor performance was strikingly enhanced following sleep.

So, athletic teens need to train well but also sleep well and long. If they train too much they'll get fatigued and lose functionality. And if they don't get enough rest after training—just like with book learning and all-nighters—they won't be able to perform anywhere near their best. A much better regimen is for them to train, nap if needed (see more on napping below and in Chapter 8), and then get a good night's sleep. As Dr. Robert Stickgold, a key researcher on sleep-dependent learning, states, "It's practice, with sleep, that makes perfect."

Auditory Learning
The sleeping brain doesn't only take on tough motor-related learning. It's also spectacular at enabling complex auditory, or hearing-based, learning. This type of learning normally develops over an extended period, and studies show that sleep provides improvement for several

days after the information is taken in. Sleep's effect is particularly evident in the effort and attention that are needed to perform a difficult sound-based task—the effort is reduced and the person is better able to pay attention to the sound stimulus.

Learning a new language is a difficult task that depends on sleep. It involves the acquisition of several different skills, including the ability to articulate a word in the same way that you hear it, make proper word choices, and remember the new vocabulary. These fact-based skills, and other skills involved with learning a language, have been shown to improve with both REM and slow wave sleep—and are critical to your teen's academic performance. They're also key to her learning the lines for the school play, remembering the words or music to a favorite song, and playing a passage on the guitar or piano.

Visual Learning

Your ability to discriminate visually also improves with sleep; studies have shown that sight-based skills improve through sleep but do not improve over the same number of hours of wakefulness. In a study of participants' ability to discriminate among textures, it was found that more and different brain regions were activated during sleep than during a similar time period of wakefulness—and that the participants who slept performed the tasks more successfully the next day.

Postsleep visual-learning improvement is something you can see for yourself—and your teen can see it with you. Find a book of word search puzzles or look for some online (the Web site www.free-online-word-search-puzzles.com offers a number of puzzles you can try, on such topics as cinema/TV, sports, the English language, science, and music). To work the puzzles, look for words that are hidden in the grid of letters. Words will be found going up, down, forward, backward, and diagonally, and in some puzzles a letter will be part of two or more words.

Once you locate a puzzle, see how many words you can find. Then get a good night's sleep and try it again the next day. Over a several-day period, with plenty of rest, you'll most likely find that you do better and better and better.

You can also test sleep's positive visual-learning effect by doing

Letter	A	B	C	D	E	F	G	H	I	K	L	M	N	O	R	S	T	W	Y
Code	1	X	7	P	9	J	7	L	E	L	4	Z	2	6	Q	3	G	S	E

H O L D   ·   F A S T   ·   T O   ·   D R E A M S

F O R   I F   D R E A M S   D I E

L I F E   ·   I S   A   ·   B R O K E N

W I N G E D   B I R D   T H A T

C A N N O T   F L Y

Try this test of sustained attention, concentration, and memory when you are well rested and when you are sleep deprived by using the code across the top to encode this saying. You may time yourself for completing the entire task or give yourself two minutes and see how much you can complete.

crossword puzzles or other kinds of word puzzles. A number of word games are available at www.shockwave.com; if you go to www.shockwave.com/sw/content/texttwist you can download a free trial of a game that will keep a history of 11 games so that you can see how you improve each time you sleep on it.

Aiding Creativity and Problem Solving

In addition to benefiting learning in all of its forms, a 2004 German study provided firm evidence that adequate sleep is linked directly to creativity and problem-solving ability. Scientists at the University of Lubeck discovered that study participants who slept for eight hours before taking a math test were three times more likely to figure out the right answers than participants who had stayed awake all night. The participants had to follow two rules in order to transform strings of eight-digit numbers into a new string and discover a third rule that was hidden in the pattern. When participants performed the calculations after sleeping, the scientists saw proof that their sleeping brains had continued to work on the problem.

The leader of the study said that the reorganizing and refining of memories during the night appeared to enhance creativity as well as problem solving. In another study a night of sleep was shown to more than double the likelihood of discovering an innovative solution to a math problem. Scientists who study the link between sleep and creativity believe that both slow wave sleep and REM sleep dreams are associated with the creative process.

One final fact here that applies not only to math but to every other subject: The National Sleep Foundation reports that a sleep-deprived person can memorize facts but will be unable to use the information in an innovative way.

Can Napping Help?

At least eight and a half, and ideally nine and a half, hours of sleep is what your teen needs to log every night in order to achieve high-level learning. But, you may be wondering, can napping every day fill in for the nighttime sleep that's missing? We'll cover napping in depth in Chapter 8, where I'll tell you more about why I don't usually encourage teens to nap (it keeps their sleep phase delay operational), but here I will say that if a full eight or nine hours isn't in the cards, a nap will help some with learning and function. However, I don't recommend napping on a regular basis, just for those times when it's absolutely required to prevent total shutdown.

IT'S A FACT

Sleep deprivation has a huge negative effect not only on the areas of learning covered here but on all aspects of learning. According to the National Sleep Foundation, it impairs

- Your ability to pay attention
- Effective communication
- Abstract thinking
- Mental sharpness
- Decision making involved in the unexpected
- Adaptive learning, which involves retrieving knowledge from long-term memory, adding to that knowledge, and using it to solve problems
- Overall motivation to learn

5

Trying to Sleep in a No-Sleep Teen Culture

Earlier in the book I talked about one of the primary reasons teens have trouble getting the sleep they need: They're biologically cued to fall asleep much later at night than adults and younger children. That biological factor is enormous on its own, but layered over it, compounding the problem, are social and cultural factors that are also working to keep your teen in a permanent sleep-deprived haze. All of these influences are important to understand, and some of them may truly surprise you.

Early School Start Times

I've already mentioned the negative impact of early school start times, and I'll go further into its effects on sleep and learning as well as what you can do to change start times in Chapter 13. But here I want to say briefly that it's one of the key reasons so many teens aren't able to live and perform to their potential.

Many parents, including me and possibly you, started middle school and high school somewhere around 8:00 or 8:30 or even later in the morning—and it seemed like an enormous challenge to get there on time. But approximately 12 to 15 years ago, school start times started creeping even closer to the cock's crow. Now it's not unusual for classes to begin at 7:20, which, for the many kids who have sports practice before school, take the bus, or need to drive or bicycle a fair distance to school, means getting up before the sun. And that of course means very little sleep if they weren't able to fall asleep before midnight.

What's driven this change in start times? In a word, money. Ever-increasing financial pressures have caused schools to make changes that will save them cash, and one of those changes involved transportation. School districts have found that it's less expensive if the same buses and drivers bring all the students to school, rather than have separate buses and drivers for each school, and that the only way to do that is to get the buses started early, which means classes must start early as well. Getting kids to school early also helps reduce rush-hour traffic, which makes businesses and municipalities surrounding the schools very happy.

But it doesn't make teens happy, or healthy, or high performing. Certainly the powers that be who made the start-time changes didn't mean to cause students harm—they only wanted to improve the district's bottom line. But it turned out that earlier start times negatively affect teens—by depriving them of precious sleep. As you read in the previous chapters, not sleeping through four to five cycles of all five sleep stages—which you can't do if you're sleeping only from midnight to 6:00 a.m.—keeps teens not only performing at a lower level but learning at a lower level. That change of one to one and a half hours in start time has had an enormous, damaging effect.

School, Home, Social, and Future Life Pressures

Everyone has to deal with pressure, of course, but teens do get a big dose of it pretty much everywhere they turn—and that keeps them up at night worrying. In their social lives, which are enormously important to them, there is pressure to fit in, know what's going on, and stay in close touch with friends. At home, their parents are constantly urging them to study more and participate in activities so they'll be accepted by a selective college, as well as help out with family responsibilities. And of course high school is one giant pressure cooker. There teens not only need to keep on top of hours and hours of classes and homework, plus pass standardized and exit tests, but they must think ahead to college too.

Having college on the horizon brings on even more pressure. Of course, there are the SATs and the ACTs, as well as making sure you're taking classes on the college track. But many high school counselors and college admissions officers tell students that colleges would rather see them get a B or even a C in an honors or an advanced placement class than an A in a less rigorous class. This information can push kids who can't handle that kind of work into taking the more difficult classes—and feeling the increased pressure and pain.

Colleges also say they want applicants who have shown steady improvement over the high school years, which again may cause kids to take on more than they comfortably can. Some of the patients I see are taking four advanced placement classes along with several other classes and are participating in a full load of activities. They're loathe to give anything up when I suggest it because they think it would damage their college chances. The college-related pressure is strong and builds from freshman through senior year.

A TEEN'S TAKE

"Yes, high school is a lot of pressure. I'm not always up late at night worrying about what the next day will bring, but there are some nights when things do weigh heavily on my mind, like when I have multiple papers due, tests, or I've had a fight with a friend or a boyfriend. The pressure comes from a lot of places. Teachers try to pressure you, close to the breaking point, and I have a ton of friends who feel they have to stay up late and finish their work to please their parents. Other people, like me, put the pressure on themselves. Wherever it comes from, it's pretty destructive."

That pressure can actually accelerate during senior year if students apply to colleges on the early-decision basis. Counselors often tell students that applying under this option gives them a better chance of being accepted, and it does give them at least a statistical advantage. But applying in this way can really stress kids out. Not only do they have to gather all the application materials and write several essays when fall classes are just starting, plus face a stronger pool of applicants, but if they're accepted they're bound to attend that college when they may not have had enough time to think through their choice.

While teens often put pressure on themselves to meet their own and everyone else's expectations regarding college, parents can sometimes unknowingly put pressure on them, too. We all want our kids to do their best, but when we hear how competitive colleges have become, because there are more outstanding students than openings in a freshman class, we can get caught up in the hysteria. Baby Boomer parents in particular, whose own parents were thrilled that their kids could go to any college, are eager for their teens to attend the most selective colleges and, later, graduate schools. So while there are many wonderful colleges out there, and because a college should be chosen because it's a great match for the student's interests and abilities, teens often feel pressured to go to one of the handful of top-rated schools.

LOWERING THE PRESSURE

One Maryland high school held a parents' night to ease some of the college pressure. During one presentation, the college counselor wrote on a blackboard the names of a number of well-known, successful people, from politicians to CEOs to authors to TV broadcasters. Then he asked the parents what those people had in common—and it turned out that none of them had gone to an Ivy League college. The point, of course, was that there are many, many colleges and universities that produce outstanding, successful alumni and that parents can ease the pressure by encouraging their kids to choose a college that's right for them.

After-School Activities and Job Pressure

Academic pressure is certainly fierce for many kids. But in addition to that pressure, many adolescents face the pressure that comes with participating in sports, being involved in community service programs and other activities, and holding down after-school and weekend jobs. Many kids, of course, take part in extracurricular activities because of interest and talent, but as they move through their high school years they're often pressured into staying with those activities to show expertise and experience on their college application forms. If interests change or time is tight, kids may want to give something up but worry that if they do they'll be hurting their chances of being accepted by the college of their choice. The result can be more sleepless nights as well as bitten nails.

Jobs, too, can be a source of worry as well as exhaustion. Many kids all over the world need to add to the family income by working after school, but working teens can't start their homework until later in the evening and may have to stay up late to finish it. For some kids it's a triple whammy—on top of being perpetually tired, they worry about holding on to their job and maintaining the grades to graduate, and that anxiety can cause them still more sleep loss. When teens come to me exhausted from trying to do too much, I usually recommend that they give up their jobs unless it would financially burden their family.

IT'S A FACT

According to the U.S. Department of Labor's *Report on the Youth Labor Force*, in 2000 over 57 percent of interviewed youths reported having held some sort of job at the age of 14. Over 64 percent of the youths worked in a job when they were 15. Eighteen percent of the 14-year-olds worked either during the school year or during both the school year and the summer; 31 percent of the 15-year-olds had jobs that included working during the school year.

Sports programs, too, can deprive students of needed rest. Not only can the daily practices and games push doing homework into the wee hours, but the games are often played a good distance from home, which can leave even less time for schoolwork and sleep. My older daughter Stella found this out when she joined her college's sailing team; some of the weekend meets were held several states away, requiring a seven-hour drive each way. Though she loved the sport, during sailing season her weekends left her little time for relaxing, and she had to stay up late into the night on Sundays to finish assignments due on Monday morning.

All of this doesn't mean, of course, that you should encourage your kids not to play sports. On the contrary, it's great for their health, and can do a lot to stabilize their mood and make them feel good

Sleep researcher Mary Carskadon notes that extended travel by sports teams can be particularly hard on teams that play on the opposite coast. West Coast athletes playing in the east might not be able to fall asleep until later on the night before a game and not get enough sleep to play well. East Coast teams that play in the west will have an advantage over their opponents if they play early in the day because they'll have been awake longer and have more energy; however, when they return home, especially if they've been gone a week or more, they may have a significant phase delay that will keep them from falling asleep until late. While adults who travel from coast to coast can experience problems adjusting to the different time zones, teens are at a greater disadvantage because of their different inner clocks.

about themselves. But if your teen is a serious athlete, it's a good idea to be aware of how much time is devoted to practices and meets and make sure she isn't overextended and dangerously sleep deprived.

The Need for Privacy and Personal Time

With their lives crammed full with classes, homework, after-school activities, jobs, social events, and family time, today's teens are busy from the moment they get out of bed until the moment they climb back in. That leaves them with no time to relax, reflect, or have a good heart to heart with a friend—all vital during the emotionally charged, change-filled teen years. So teens who are especially busy but have a strong need for time to themselves often see the hours after their family is asleep as the only time they can call their own.

That time may be used for just about anything. Some teens use it to call or IM their friends. Others like to read, write in journals, or listen to music. Still others use the time to work on a hobby. After a hectic day, quiet time, when no one's asking anything of them and they can actually relax, can be very appealing to adolescents—and worth the exhaustion that results the next day.

Another reason teens choose to stay up late at night is because they can. It's not only quiet after midnight, but it's a time over which they can have some control. After a day that's regimented by school administrators, teachers, coaches, and parents, the night hours are a time when kids can be in charge. For independent-minded teens, who are working to break away and find their own identity, time that they can regulate can seem like a must-have.

Three Patients Say . . .

❝I get to have a secret relationship with myself when everyone goes to bed around midnight. I get to think and write and get to know my own mind in a very honest environment. **❞**

❝I have two friends who I'm never able to see during the day [at college]. So we meet quietly at night in one of our dark dorm rooms when our roommates are asleep. We whisper and talk for hours. **❞**

❝My house is especially crazy and hectic. Nighttime is relaxing. It's just you and your thoughts. **❞**

Technology

OK, I have to warn you here—I'm about to rant and rave. Television is malignant—there's no other way to say it. The shows that adolescents watch are filled with violence, inappropriate sex, and truly horrific stuff, and it's not only warping their psyches during the day but keeping them up at night.

While some kids try to relax by watching soap operas in the afternoon—bad enough in itself—many are watching shows with disturbing content at night, right before they try to fall asleep. From 10:00 to 11:00 p.m., most networks provide programming in which characters get blown up or tied up or have life-threatening illnesses or creepy people stalking them. At a time when kids should be trying to wind down and empty their minds of problems to make the transition to sleep, they're bombarded by frightening images.

NEGATIVE EFFECTS OF TELEVISION WATCHING

The results of a research study entitled "The Children in the Community" reported in the *Archives of Pediatrics & Adolescent Medicine* showed that adolescents who watched more than three hours of TV a day were at a significantly higher risk for sleep problems by early adulthood. Adolescents who lowered their TV watching to less than an hour a day experienced a significant reduction in that risk.

Much of what's on TV at night just doesn't make viewers feel good. And if you're already worried or feeling under pressure, a heavy dose of suspense can send you over the edge. But these shows can be very hard to turn off because their formats are calculated to have you watch until the next commercial, and you feel like you can't shut them off before the end. And if teens have a TV in their room, they may be even less likely to turn the thing off—and you'll be less likely to know what they're watching and less likely to ask them to turn it off. While I know many teens think of TV watching as a way to relax, I believe it's counterproductive and adds to their sleep issues.

MORE NEGATIVE EFFECTS OF TELEVISION WATCHING

In a study noted in MediaFamily.org's online MediaWise column, 65 percent of teens reported having a television in their bedrooms. And according to a study conducted by the National Institute on Media and the Family, kids who have a TV in their room watch five and a half hours more TV each week than kids who don't. Not only has this extensive exposure to television been linked to poor school performance, it contributes to reducing kids' desire to become involved in nonelectronic activities, such as reading, outings, and family time.

Computers, too, can be very stimulating and add to teens' sleep problems. Yes, kids need them for homework and projects, but if they browse the Internet or spend time on disturbing Web sites or playing violent computer games close to lights out—or after lights out—it will be a big deterrent to winding down enough to sleep. At my home we keep the computers in the family room so that it's less likely that my kids will browse inappropriate sites or e-mail or IM friends in the middle of the night. It also helps to keep some of the homework materials off their beds and out of their rooms and makes it more likely that, when they go to their bedrooms, sleep will actually take place.

Then, of course, in addition to the MP3 players and all the other portable music options, there are the ubiquitous cell phones. I certainly use mine every day and I imagine you use yours, but I don't

IT'S A FACT

A recent study by the Pew Internet & American Life Project found that 81 percent of teens who use the Internet play games online and 75 percent use Instant Messaging—35 percent of whom say they IM for over an hour a day. If there's no time for it during the daylight and evening hours because of busy schedules, I wonder when there is time . . .

think you and I use ours in the middle of the night—the way many teens do. Adolescent patients tell me that they often talk on their cell phones or text message under the covers, making plans with friends for the next day or finding out about any social happenings they missed that day. They may stay up chatting for hours, and when they do finally try to get some rest, any worrisome news they heard, about their boy-

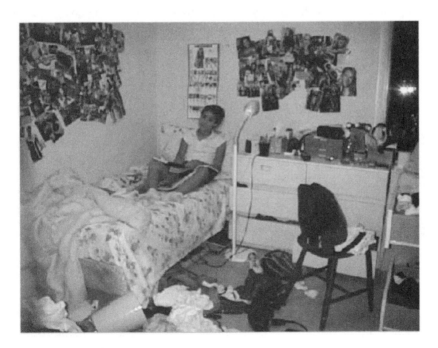

Look familiar? The many distractions of the adolescent bedroom.

friend or girlfriend or even schoolwork, can make them too anxious to fall asleep.

If they do fall asleep, there still may be another problem—many teens don't turn their cell phones off at night and keep them in their rooms, if not right in bed with them. Remember the story I told you earlier about how Elyssa's cell phone rang at 2:00 a.m. when she and I were on a college tour? Well, she's not the only teen receiving phone calls when the callers—and everyone else—should be sleeping. (If you don't think this is a problem at your house, ask your cell phone service provider for an itemized bill; you might be amazed to see the hours at which your teen is receiving—or making—calls.)

To cut down on this sleep-reducing problem, I encourage patients to either turn their phones off at night or leave them in the kitchen or another room away from their bedroom. They can check their messages first thing in the morning, the way Elyssa does, and get right back to social business then. It's even possible, if your teen's friends or her parents read this book, or your teen knows that you know that she's making calls after lights out, that there might not be any middle-of-the-night messages to answer.

It's a Status Symbol

While many teens learn that staying up well past midnight exhausts them and that they need to get more sleep, others think that the later they stay up, the better. Yes, they may be perpetually tired and their academics, sports, and social lives may suffer, but to them staying up all night is a sign that they're tough and cool, that they can handle anything. Some kids even have contests to see who can stay awake the longest. One patient told me, "I beat my friend in our staying-awake contest when he fell asleep at 5:00 a.m. the next day. He tried to deny it, but we had him on film. He had to buy me dinner."

It's a Low Priority

When teens are loaded down with school, work, and activities, and they realize that something's got to give, it's often sleep—getting eight or nine hours of the stuff just isn't at the top of the list. Adolescents who want to do it all—and that's many of them—believe that eliminating some sleep will give them more time for what they want and are expected to accomplish. That, of course, backfires, because getting less rest makes them less energetic and more stressed, but still they often make the choice to sleep less so that they can do more.

A Bad Mood

Just think about how pumped up you need to be to get through a hectic day and then do it all over again the next. And think how stressed you feel when you're under pressure to perform, perform, perform. Teens who aren't sleeping well or long enough can get worn down by the constant need to stay in the game and smile—and it can put them in a perpetually bad mood. That in turn can add to their sleeplessness and make them feel bad about themselves—and that can make them want to stay up late so they can talk with their friends and feel better. During the day, when that pressure is actively on them, just looking at their parents can make teens feel it more; late at night, when the reminders aren't visible, teens can socialize, relax, and feel free to enjoy themselves.

Living in a Multitasking World

Multitasking may seem like a strange thing to keep teens awake. But most teens today operate at a fairly complex level, and the hectic day-time schedules they keep can actually cause them problems at night. Even when she watches TV, Elyssa multitasks by talking on the phone with friends and maybe getting things ready for the next day; some kids watch TV, listen to music through headsets, and do their home-work all at the same time. After keeping all their many balls in the air during the day and packing in as many leisure-time activities as pos-sible in the evening, many kids find it hard to let go at night and sleep. And some kids who are busy and connected all day can actually feel lonely at night, which makes them worry and stay awake, too.

Consuming Caffeine

Ah, caffeine. It's what many adults rely on to get their motor running every morning. But as I talked about in Chapter 2, too much of the

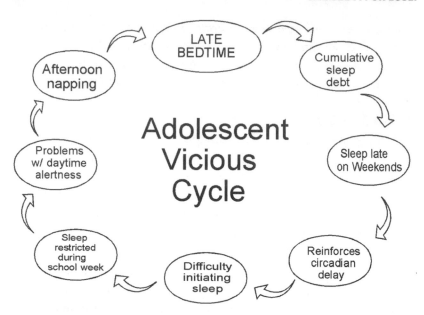

Details of the vicious cycle of late sleep time, insufficient sleep, and late weekend sleep-ins that our teens are dealing with.

stuff late in the day can keep you awake late into the night. Caffeine intake has also been associated with worsening mood.

Many teens, though, especially those in college, like to get together in the evening to relax or study over a cup of coffee or tea. And, of course, what's better to have with coffee or tea than a rich, chocolaty dessert or giant chocolate chip cookie? On a warm night coffee or tea might be replaced with an ice-cold cola—but most of those choices are packed with a big dose of caffeine too. (See page 43 for the caffeine content of many popular beverages.)

So teens might drink caffeine in the morning to cope with their sleep deprivation, drink more to get their schoolwork done, and then consume more in the evening when they get together or study with friends—which will make them feel grumpier and grumpier and feed the continuing sleep deprivation cycle. And if they feel bad enough as they try to accomplish all they need to do, they just might turn to an even more powerful form of caffeine in the mistaken hope of feeling and performing better. A high-caffeine drink called Bawls, which is currently advertised to Internet game players, is marketed with the slogan "Who needs sleep? Drink Bawls. Never sleep."

Parents

Uh, oh, here's one antisleep influence you probably didn't want to see. I alluded to it earlier when I talked about how parents get caught up in the college hysteria and contribute to the pressure weighing on their teen. But the truth is, parents add to their teen's sleeplessness in other ways: The current generation of parents of teens is not great at respecting their own sleep needs, so they're setting a poor example for their kids as well as sometimes failing to set limits for them.

Just as we need to set a good example in other areas of healthy living, we parents need to model good sleep habits as well as guide our kids to get more and better sleep. These twin goals are so important, in fact, that I've devoted two separate chapters to the issues: Chapter 8 covers techniques that will help you help your teen establish her own successful sleep program, and Chapter 12 discusses how you can become a great sleep role model.

Briefly, though, I want to note here that while your teen may look like she's completely ignoring you and everything you say (you know that look), she knows exactly what you do and hears quite well what you say—she just might choose not to acknowledge it. But if she sees you staying up late , she'll think that must be OK. If she sees you drinking coffee to get moving, she's likely to down a lot of java too. If you're a couch potato, she might become one as well—and on and on and on. I'm certainly not saying that you shouldn't watch TV or multitask or work late if you need to, but I encourage you to be aware of the household dynamic in which your teen is growing up.

Part II

How to Help Teens Feel and Be Their Best

6

Off the Charts:
Measuring Teen Sleepiness

Not long ago, when I walked out to my clinic's reception area to greet my next patient, I found her sitting with a magazine on her lap—fast asleep. From her bedraggled look—hair uncombed, shirt button missing, belongings scattered at her feet—and her ability to fall asleep in a noisy waiting room in the middle of the afternoon, I was pretty sure she was a youngster with a major case of sleep deprivation.

But she didn't agree. When we chatted in my office and I asked her why she had come to see me, she said her pediatrician had sent her because she hadn't found anything that would account for the moodiness and drop in grades that her parents were worried about. But Mara herself was sure nothing was wrong. She told me she felt perfectly fine and wasn't sleepy at all.

As part of her evaluation, I asked Mara to keep a sleep log (see page 133 for a sample of my sleep log) and come to my sleep lab to take a daytime napping test. And, lo and behold, the results showed that Mara was not just sleepy but pathologically sleepy.

Why didn't she know this? And why couldn't her parents or her pediatrician recognize it?

A big problem with sleep deprivation is that it's not always easy to spot—either by the person who's experiencing it, like Mara, or by the people in that person's life. And that goes for adults as well as adolescents and younger kids. As far as teenagers go, sometimes some of the symptoms—such as being moody or falling behind in school or being sleepy—are attributed to rebelliousness or laziness or typical adolescent behavior, not an underlying physical cause. And some sleep-deprived people just function better than others, doing fairly well though definitely not their best. Younger adolescents don't always have the judgment to understand that being sleep deprived is interfering with their lives. Others who are severely sleep deprived may have additional problems that mask or share symptoms with sleep deprivation, such as attention deficit disorder (ADD) or depression, and that makes it extremely difficult to diagnose them. (For more on the links between sleep deprivation and ADD and depression, see Chapter 11.)

So how can you tell if your teen is truly sleep deprived—and to what degree?

There are several ways to tell. If you think your teen has a sleep problem, you can send her to her doctor. If your teen checks out well there, and no other medical condition is found, an evaluation by a sleep specialist like me will provide valuable information. (To find a certified sleep specialist in your area, search under "Patient Resources" on the American Academy of Sleep Medicine's Web site, www.aasmnet.org. Your local medical society should also be a good resource for sleep doctors in your community.)

You can also gather and assess important information yourself, along with your teen. This chapter includes a number of sleepiness tests and scales as well as a description of typical symptoms to look for to help you make a determination. You'll also find several Web site addresses where your teen can test herself on sleep-dependent performance. And I'll give you some ideas for informal tests you can create yourself.

What Does a Tired Teen Look and Act Like?

Some of the more obvious signs of sleep deprivation may already be pretty clear to you—you see them in yourself as well as your teen. There are the bags under the eyes, the constant yawning, the dozing off at inappropriate times. But many sleep deficit symptoms are not quite so recognizable. For instance, we talked in Chapter 2 about the fact that many exhausted teens get headaches, but if you hadn't read that chapter you probably wouldn't have thought, "Lots of headaches. It could be sleep deprivation."

To give you a better picture of what a sleep-deprived teen might look like, the following list names the top 13 symptoms my adolescent patients exhibit:

- Yawning
- Falling asleep at inappropriate times
- Trouble getting out of bed in the morning
- Taking more than 20 minutes to fall asleep at night
- Frequent headaches
- Sallow skin
- Bags under the eyes
- Irritability bordering on hostility
- Clumsiness
- Lack of verbal output (doesn't talk very much)
- Doesn't respond to questions (I have to repeat them)
- Sullenness
- Has a low mood or is depressed (occasionally the opposite, giddiness, can be seen)

In addition, many adolescent patients' grades deteriorate, and they're also often tardy or absent from school. (Luckily, some school administrators and counselors now associate sleep deprivation with reduced school performance and absenteeism and recommend that chronically tardy and underperforming students seek help. However, recently I saw an 11th grader who had been arrested for truancy despite his mom calling to report that he was home asleep.)

Even knowing all this, though, it can be hard to tell if your teen is exhibiting some of the symptoms because of teens' outstanding ability to mask themselves with their makeup and fashion statements. But here a photo can help. Take a look at a photo of your teen from a year

One Teen Says . . .

❝*During the school year I get about five hours of sleep a night. I set my alarm for 5:30 so that I have enough time to shower and get my hair and makeup all set before the bus comes. I'm really out when I sleep, though, so I set seven different alarm clocks all over the room. I usually don't hear the first couple, and then when I start to hear them I wait until the seventh one goes off so that I can stay in bed until the last second.* ❞

---

or two ago and compare it to one from today. Does the older picture show a bright-eyed and bright-skinned youngster? Does it show an adolescent bursting with energy and actually smiling for the camera? Even if the clothes worn for the photo were baggy or sported colors that made you want to avert your eyes, was your teen fairly well groomed and pulled together?

Showing your teen the two photos might be helpful to her understanding of a potential sleep problem as well. And looking at two other photos might make a light bulb go off, too. Try taking a photo of your teen—or encourage your youngster to take one—on the day after a night of little sleep. Take another on a day after your teen has logged at least eight hours of sleep or even after a weekend night of 10 hours of sleep (the more, of course, the better). The difference may be startling—and an eye opener. Your teen might also be interested in comparing photos of friends under the same circumstances or taking photos of friends and trying to guess how much sleep they got the night before.

Using Professional Sleepiness Assessment Tools

Looking closely at your teen and thinking carefully about her behavior will go a long way in helping you decide if there is a possible sleep problem. But professional measurements can be extremely useful too. In my practice I use a number of sleepiness scales and questionnaires to help me make a determination, and I'm including some of them here so that you can use them as well.

Adolescent Sleepiness Scale

The Adolescent Sleepiness Scale is a 10-point subjective assessment of alertness.* It's particularly useful because it asks teens to determine how hard it is to stay awake while doing typical activities such as reading and talking with friends or teachers. The test can be repeated at intervals to check your teen's progress in getting more rest.

Adolescent Sleepiness Scale

During the last two weeks, have you struggled to stay awake (fought sleep) or fallen asleep in the following situations? (Mark 1 answer for every item.)

1 = No
2 = Struggled to stay awake
3 = Fallen asleep
4 = Both struggled to stay awake and have fallen asleep

1. In a face-to-face conversation with another person?

2. Traveling in a bus, train, plane, or car?

3. Attending a performance (movie, concert, or play)?

4. Watching television or listening to the radio or stereo?

5. Reading, studying, or doing homework?

6. During a test?

7. In a class at school?

8. While doing work on a computer?

9. Playing video games?

10. Driving a car?

Do you drive?

SOURCE: Wofson AR, Carskadon MA, et al. Evidence for the validity of a sleep habits survey for adolescents. Sleep 26(2):213-216, 2003. See www.sleepforscience.org for the entire Sleep Habits Survey.

Scoring

A total score over 10 should be reviewed carefully, with all positive responses evaluated. A score between 15 and 20 signals a significant degree of daytime sleepiness and should alert you and your teen that she needs to get more sleep.

The Epworth Sleepiness Scale

This scientifically validated measure of sleepiness* is used widely to assess adult daytime sleepiness over the past week or so. You can answer the questionnaire yourself, to get an idea of your own sleepiness level in an effort to lower it, or encourage your 20-something daughter to fill in the blanks. There are eight questions with a 24-point scale.

Epworth Sleepiness Scale

How likely are you to doze off or fall asleep in the following situations?
Answer considering how you have felt over the past week or so.

0 = Would never doze
1 = Slight chance of dozing
2 = Moderate chance of dozing
3 = High chance of dozing

1. Sitting and reading	
2. Watching TV	
3. Sitting inactive in a public place (e.g., theater or meeting)	
4. As a passenger in a car for an hour without a break	
5. Lying down to rest in the afternoon when able	
6. Sitting and talking to someone	
7. Sitting quietly after a lunch without alcohol	
8. In a car while stopped for a few minutes in traffic	

*SOURCE: Johns MR. A new method of measuring daytime sleepiness: The Epworth Sleepiness Scale. Sleep 14(6):540-545, 1991. Reproduced with permission.

Scoring
1–7: You're getting enough sleep
8–9: You're borderline
10 or higher: You're sleepy

Stanford Sleepiness Scale

Another way to evaluate daytime sleepiness is with the Stanford Sleepiness Scale.* Rather than assessing how sleepy you've felt over

Stanford Sleepiness Scale

Using the scale below, indicate the single number that best describes your level of alertness or sleepiness at each time:

1 = Feeling actrive, vital, alert, or wide awake
2 = Functioning at high levels, but not at peak; able to concentrate
3 = Relaxed, awake but not fully alert; responsive
4 = A little foggy
5 = Foggy, beginning to lose track; having difficulty staying awake
6 = Sleepy, woozy, fighting sleep; prefer to lie down
7 = Cannot stay awake, sleep onset appears imminent

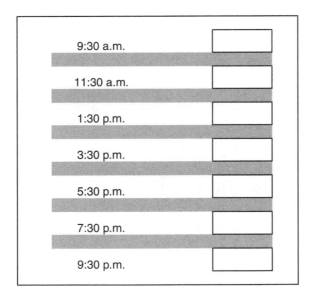

SOURCE: Hoddes E, Zarcone V, Smythe H, et al. Quantification of sleepiness: A new approach. Psychophysiology 10:431-436, 1973.

Pediatric Daytime Sleepiness Scale*

Please answer the following questions as honestly as you can:

	Always	Frequently	Sometimes	Seldom	Never
1. How often do you fall asleep or get drowsy during class periods?	4	3	2	1	0
2. How often do you get sleepy or drowsy while doing your homework?	4	3	2	1	0
3. Are you usually alert most of the day?	0	1	2	3	4
4. How often are you ever tired and grumpy during the day?	4	3	2	1	0
5. How often do you have trouble getting out of bed in the morning?	4	3	2	1	0
6. How often do you fall back to sleep after being awakened in the morning?	4	3	2	1	0
7. How often do you need someone to awaken you in the morning?	4	3	2	1	0
	Very often	Often	Sometimes	Seldom	Never
8. How often do you think that you need more sleep?	4	3	2	1	0

*SOURCE: Drake, C, Nickel, C, Burduvali, E. The Pediatric Daytime Sleepiness Scale (PDSS): Sleep habits and school outcomes in middle-school children. Sleep 26(4):455-458, 2003.

the past few days or weeks, however, this test checks how alert or tired you feel every few hours during one day. The test can be taken by both adults and adolescents and provides information about how your alertness varies during different times of the day. It also points out the most problematic times of the day. If you like, you can rate your teen later in the evening to get a sense of how late her internal clock is delayed, but you can take the test at any time and as frequently as you like. I've found that rating yourself every two hours provides a good picture of how your daytime alertness varies.

Scoring

Ideally you want a rating of 1 for every test. But remember that people entrained to the normal day-night cycle typically feel less alert in the mid- to late afternoon. Any score higher than 3 indicates that you may be seriously sleepy.

The Pediatric Daytime Sleepiness Scale

The Pediatric Daytime Sleepiness Scale (PDSS) was created to meet the need for a sleepiness measurement for elementary and middle school children. Students between the ages of 11 and 15 were first studied to determine the relationship between daytime sleepiness and school performance, and the scale is now widely used to question sixth, seventh, and eighth graders about their sleep habits. While the scale has not been validated for older teens and students in their early twenties, it's a good way to see how sleepy younger teens are. It's also helpful for catching sleep deficits from which your younger children suffer before poor habits become ingrained. Repeat the test as often as you like to measure your young teen's progress.

Scoring

When the PDSS test was first given to sixth through eighth graders, there was a clear correlation between higher scores and worse academic performance, worse mood, and especially anger and more frequent illness. In that sample, sixth graders had an average score of 11.8; seventh graders, 12.9; and eighth graders, 13.8. Scores above these averages signal that a young teen may have a sleep problem. A score of 16 or higher is likely to be associated with a negative impact on daily functioning.

Using Additional Professional Assessment Tools

In addition to using the assessment tools in the previous section, you and your teen can gather important information with tests that measure what are often sleepiness-related conditions. Three tests are included here: one that measures the ability to pay attention, one that measures headache occurrence, and one that identifies symptoms of depression (for more on the link between these and other conditions and sleep deprivation, see Chapter 11).

The Divided-Attention Test

Because sleep-impaired teens can resemble alcohol-impaired teens—Chapter 2 noted that sleep deprivation produces psychomotor response impairments equivalent to those caused by consuming alcohol at or above the legal limit and that, after teens are awake for more than 16 hours, they drive as though they had a blood-alcohol level of 0.05 to 0.1 percent—I'm including this test developed by the National Highway Traffic Safety Administration. Used to determine whether drivers are driving drunk, the test includes physical exercises that sober people can easily perform. It's called the Divided-Attention Test because the exercises require test takers to divide their attention between listening to and following instructions and doing certain physical movements—something with which a sleep-deprived person will have difficulty.

There are two parts to the test:

• The Walk-and-Turn Test, which asks test takers to take nine steps, heel to toe, in a straight line, then turn on one foot and walk in the same manner in the opposite direction
• The One-Leg Stand Test, in which test takers stand with one foot about six inches off the ground and count out loud by thousands (1,001, 1,002, etc.) until they're told to put their foot down, usually about 30 seconds

Scoring

In the Walk-and-Turn Test, police officers look for seven signs of impairment:

- Can't keep balance while listening to the instructions
- Begins before the instructions are finished
- Stops while walking to regain balance
- Does not touch heel to toe
- Uses arms to keep balance
- Loses balance while turning
- Takes the wrong number of steps

In the One-Leg Stand Test, officers look for four signs of impairment:

- Swaying while balancing
- Using arms to balance
- Hopping to maintain balance
- Putting down the foot

In both tests, 65 to 68 percent of test takers who exhibit two or more signs of impairment have a blood alcohol level of 0.10 or greater. Sleep-deprived teens will likely be impaired to a similar degree and experience a serious reduction in motor response time.

Evaluating Headaches

As I've mentioned already, and will go into detail about in Chapter 11, headaches frequently accompany sleepiness. To help distinguish between sleep deprivation headaches and more serious migraines, I recommend that you encourage your teen to take the quiz at www.headachequiz.com. You can also ask your teen to check out the symptoms of migraines below. If you suspect your teen has migraines, consult her doctor and pay careful attention to her sleep needs.

Symptoms Suggestive of Migraine Headaches

Visual disturbance: jagged or zigzag lines, reflective appearance, shimmering, flashing lights, or peripheral or central loss of vision

Headaches that involve only one side of the head
Nausea or vomiting
Sensitivity to light or sound
Pounding or throbbing sensation
Speech disturbance
Numbness, tingling, or weakness

Depression Screening

Tired adolescents often exhibit a low mood as well as decreased interest in schoolwork and activities—which may be signs of depression. To help sort out sleepiness from depression, take a look at the depression screening test developed by the New York University Medical Center, which is available online at www.med.nyu.edu/psych/screens/depres.html. (Do remember, though, that having symptoms of depression does not necessarily mean you have depression.) If your teen's test result is negative but you still suspect she has clinical depression, be sure to have her evaluated by a professional. Depression and impulsiveness can be a lethal combination in adolescents.

Using Informal Assessment Tools

Professional measurements are definitely great sources for gathering important information on sleep deprivation—I rely on them in my practice to add to what I observe in and hear from patients. But if it's difficult for you to get your teen to take any of the tests included here, or you just want to round out your understanding with additional input, you can gather valuable information from informal sources.

Online memory games and puzzles are great—and enjoyable—ways to see how your teen's memory and reaction time stack up, helping you determine if she is sleep deprived (you remember from Chapter 4 that poor sleep can equal poor learning). The idea is to see how well your teen compares to others playing the same game and to learn how speedily she reacts during the time allowed. By playing the game several times, after a good night's sleep and after a night of little sleep, you and your teen will have evidence that sleep loss impairs performance—and that sleep deprivation is in play. (See Resources for several of my favorite Web sites that offer a variety of memory games.)

In addition to playing the Web games, you or your teen can devise memory tests of your own. For example, you could develop a list of 20 words, read them to your teen, wait 10 minutes, and then see how many words your teen can write down. Or your teen could take a timed test in which she has to come up with as many names of animals—or states or trees—as possible. Or teens could test each other on how many mental math problems they can work in a certain time period. Being able to remember only a few words or name only a few animals or do only a few problems would be a strong indication of sleep-deprived performance.

My own 12-year-old niece proved the sleep-performance link by giving fellow students at her middle school an informal memory test. As part of a science project, she read a list of 20 words to a number of students during lunch period and then tested their recall at the end of the school day. The next day she tested them again—and asked how much sleep they had gotten on each of the nights before questioning. Just as she had hypothesized, those who had slept more recalled more words.

7

Tips from Teens:
How Parents Can Talk with Their Teens
About the Importance of Sleep

If your teen scored poorly on one or more of the sleep-related tests in the previous chapter, or she complains constantly of exhaustion or headaches or any of the other sleep deprivation symptoms, it's time to start doing something about the potentially damaging condition. You may already have tried to establish better sleep and wake times for your teen, or taken other steps to improve her sleep habits, but I'm not telling you anything new when I say that it's not always easy to get teens to listen to—and follow—an adult's advice.

But teens do listen to their friends. And knowing that, I enlisted my 17-year-old daughter Elyssa to tell you about some of the ways she believes parents can get the sleep message across to their teens without getting into a huge battle. The idea is that if you know what has helped Elyssa hear the message about sleep and do things that give her more and better rest, you may be able to talk to your own teen in a similar way and, I hope, have the same positive result. Elyssa is going to tell you about how she's dealt with the problem of sleep, what I've done wrong in trying to help her get the sleep she needs (I fear there'll be a lot of that), and how you can encourage your teen to own her sleep-wake schedule.

You'll also hear in this chapter from other teens who have words of wisdom for us poor, struggling parents. Elyssa's thoughts will be detailed in a question-and-answer format and the other teens' insights will be featured in boxes.

Elyssa: Let me start out by saying that I am by no means the perfect poster child for adolescent sleep. At times I have pulled all-nighters, slept past noon, and stayed up all night talking to friends or watching TV. However, from my 17 years of sleep experience, I have discovered that to perform at my top level academically and physically, I have to get an adequate amount of sleep. Since I know how little sleep teens get—even fewer hours than their parents think, if you count the last-minute review of note cards, the magazine reading, and the secret trips to the computer in the middle of the night—I want to share my experience and knowledge to help you help my peers feel better and perhaps ease your minds in the process.

Q: What's the sleep-wake schedule you follow most of the time and do the hours you sleep keep you feeling good and doing well all day?

A: During the school year I go to sleep between 10:30 and 11:00 p.m. Sometimes I'll go to sleep earlier if I've had a long day of school plus tennis practice or a match (I play singles on my high school team) and if I don't have that much homework. But sometimes I'll go to sleep later if I have a lot of work to do that night. I wake up around 7:00 and leave the house around 7:40. On weekends and during the summer I usually go to sleep around 12:30 or sometimes 1:00, and wake up somewhere between 9:30 and 10:30. By keeping to this schedule I get the same number of hours on the weekends that I get during the week and alter my sleep-wake time by only about two hours—which my mom says keeps you from getting a phase delay further out of whack.

   Of course, there are days when I go to bed later or earlier; it all depends on what's happening the next day. Tennis lesson at 8:30 in the morning? I am in bed by 11:30 at the latest. I try to get somewhere around eight hours if I can, and I think that's the key. I know that some schools start earlier than mine, and some students have to wake up around the ungodly hour of 6:00 or 6:15, but that doesn't mean they have to go to sleep at 8:00 or 9:00. I think that as long as you are *in* bed, not signing off from Instant Messaging or brushing your teeth or anything, by 10:00, you should be fine to wake up at 6:00.

Do I feel great all day long? My goal is to wake up every morning and feel good and not be yawning all day. During the school year I almost never wake up feeling refreshed because it is just too early, but I do go through the day not feeling sleepy, so I'm happy with that. If I don't get enough sleep, I'm exhausted and unhappy.

Q: How did you figure out how much sleep you needed? Did your parents make it a rule that you had to get at least eight hours, or did you set up your own schedule?

A: Everyone has different sleep needs; some kids need more and some kids need less than others. I need more than some of my friends because I'm more active than they are. It all depends on who you are and what you do. But for a lot of teens it's just fun to stay up at night.

But my revelation about how much sleep I need wasn't forced on me by my mother—though I will say that all the years of getting the same speech from her every night about sleep somehow imprinted in my brain, so I guess that was part of it. But basically after a while I just realized on my own that around eight hours of sleep was what was healthy for me and necessary for my body.

Some of it I learned the hard way. Once I played in a tennis match that was hours away, meaning I had to get up at 6:00 a.m. to get there on time, which basically sucked. I thought I'd be fine if I got somewhere around six or seven hours of sleep—I thought a first-round match shouldn't take that much energy, plus I had gotten a whole lot of sleep for a couple of nights before. I was wrong, completely wrong. I ended up playing in a three-set match, and each match took about

---

Another Teen Says . . .

❝*A bunch of my friends think it's very romantic to stay up late. But I would tell other teens not to romanticize or dramatize the night. It's quiet and you can read and think, but then you pay for it the next day.* ❞

three hours to finish instead of the usual one hour. I was exhausted after the first match and slept for four hours before the next match—which I lost because I couldn't move.

Another time I was studying the night before a big history test, cramming like crazy. I had spent the last couple of days procrastinating, and I had convinced myself that I already knew most of it, that there wasn't that much left to cover. I sat down at my computer around 5:00 to write some study guides and within minutes I was in a panic—I freaked out because I realized there was so much information to cover.

I stayed at my computer until 12:30 easy, until I finally finished a 12-page review. But that was just the typing part—then I actually had to memorize the information. I sat on my bed with highlighters and open textbooks surrounding me, along with three cups of hot cocoa, until I finally gave up, exhausted and defeated, around 2:00 a.m. I decided I would wake up around 6:30 to review everything I had highlighted.

The next morning when I woke up I felt very unrefreshed, and I was horrified to realize that I had retained almost no information and that my test was in a matter of hours. Again panic set in. When I finally got to my classroom and my teacher started handing out the test, my eyelids drooped, my mind wandered, and that terrible feeling crept in that I didn't remember anything that I had spent the night and early morning cramming into my brain. It was not my best test, and I spent the rest of the day exhausted and feeling bad.

Why did I do this to myself? Now I know that I need to get more sleep if I'm going to play tennis at all well and do at all well at school.

Q: Were there any incentives that helped you to get more sleep, in addition to coming to the realization that you did better and felt better when you had enough rest?

A: I hate to admit it, but the arguments I had with my parents, plus my exhaustion, helped motivate me to get more sleep and take care of my body. So did waking up at 1:30 in the afternoon with 10 text messages

Another Teen Says . . .

❝ *When I was younger, my parents would take away my e-mail privileges the day after I stayed up really late IMing and didn't get enough sleep. They had the password for my account, and they had to sign me on for me to use it. That didn't always make me go to sleep earlier, but if I wanted to IM with my friends in the evenings I had to keep it in mind.* ❞

---

waiting from friends who wanted to do something with me that day that I missed out on because I slept away half the day.

But one big incentive really pushed me. At the beginning of last summer my mom and I had an argument about my sleep. School had just gotten out and I hadn't discovered a sleep pattern yet that fit me for the summer. After numerous "discussions," my mom decided that I had to have at least seven hours of sleep or I couldn't drive the car. Yeah. That made me figure out a way, really quickly, to accommodate her worries and my needs. I took the responsibility and ran with it. There was no way I was going to let car privileges be taken away if I could do something about it.

Q: What was the sleep-wake routine you used to follow that wasn't so successful for you?

A: Before I hit puberty, I went to sleep around 10 and got up for school around 7. On the weekends I could sleep till 8:30, but never any later, even though all my friends didn't wake up until around 11:00. But one summer I started sleeping later and later, and finally I was sleeping routinely until 10:30. That seemed great, but the problem was that I never wanted to go to sleep at night. When school started again, I still couldn't get to sleep, but I had to wake up early. Things didn't work out so well and I knew I had to get more sleep. Pretty quickly I got tired of being tired. My mom also nagged me to death, kept turning off the TV, and followed me to my room.

Q: Did you have specific goals in mind when you decided you needed to get more sleep? Or did you just not want to feel tired anymore? Do you recommend that teens work toward a sleep goal?

A: I didn't have any goals. In fact, I never really thought about creating a sleep schedule. But after a while I began to listen to my body and figured out what worked; I got into a pattern. My advice to parents of teens is to encourage their kids to get into some kind of routine that makes them feel healthy and happy. They should try different sleep and wake times and see what works for them, then get into a pattern and stick with it. Of course, sometimes there are going to be long nights of studying or hanging out with friends, and kids should have those—they just shouldn't make them a habit.

Q: Are your parents happy with the sleep schedule you follow most of the time? Or do they bug you to get still more sleep?

A: I'm sure that every parent wants his or her children to get more sleep. But there are only 24 hours in a day, so if your kid is getting at least eight hours of sleep, there should be no reason to nag. I hated it when my mom tried to cram bed and wake times down my throat, and I'm not sure she's mastered how to handle the situation yet. But she's learning not to force it unless it's an emergency, like I'm completely overstressed or I'm stuck in front of the TV at midnight. We want to make our parents happy, but it's not just about appeasing them.

Two Teens Agree . . .

❝ *My parents have always let me be pretty independent, so they've never imposed any time when I have to be up or go to bed. To tell the truth, sometimes I end up waking my mother when she oversleeps. My big problem is when I'm not tired but I know I need to sleep. Then it can take me forever to get to sleep no matter what I do.* **❞**

❝ *My parents do try to get me to go to bed at a decent hour. The problem is they can't make me sleep.* **❞**

Another Teen Says . . .

❝ *My parents have helped me by forcing me out of bed in the morning, but they really have helped me by respecting my need for a peaceful environment at night by keeping yelling and anxiety to a minimum.* **❞**

Q: How could your parents do a better job of helping you get enough rest? What can parents of teens in general do to argue less with their kids about sleep?

A: Well, here my mom would say that parents should read this book for good ideas, especially the ones in Chapter 8. But I can tell you a few things that my parents did that I really didn't like, and recommend that you don't do them with your kids.

I cannot tell you how many arguments my mom and I have had over my sleep. The worst thing she did that provoked an argument was to come into my room at around 10:00, when I was completely involved in my homework, and say, "Go to sleep in 15 minutes." I *hated* that. I still had things to do, maybe 30 more minutes of work, so of course that led to an argument.

I think communication is key when you want to solve a sleep issue. The best way to handle this situation if it comes up with your teen is to ask questions like, "How much more work do you have left?" This open-ended question will allow your student to make up an appropriate schedule that suits her needs. When I got my mom to ask me that, I'd tell her I had 20 more pages of reading and that I would go to sleep in 45 minutes. Easy. No arguments.

My recommendation is to try not to force your kid to go to sleep unless it's an emergency, like he or she is burning the midnight oil to finish the next day's assignments or is glued to the TV really late. This could call for drastic measures: removing the pencil from the academically crazed over-worker or shutting off the TV and having a brief "discussion" that consists of "Go to sleep now." Otherwise, talk to your teen. Ask questions. Don't make too many demands. Try to un-

Another Teen Says . . .

❝ *I get really offended when my parents try to find something to blame things on, like I didn't get enough sleep because my friend called me at 11:30. Parents always want to pin blame on something specific, but this drives teens batty. Why do parents have to find something to blame? Things are what they are.* **❞**

---

derstand where your kid is coming from so you can see her point of view.

Above all don't lecture or threaten. I personally hate being lectured about my sleep, though with a sleep doctor for a mom this is unavoidable. I do respect what she says, though, because she *is* a sleep doctor.

Q: Do you feel that kids should take on the entire responsibility of getting the rest they need and deal with the consequences if they don't get enough rest? Or should they try to work out a sleep program on which both they and their parents can agree?

A: Teenagers need to take on some of the responsibility for their sleep schedule. We aren't 10 anymore, and we don't want our mom or dad to tell us to go to bed. But to our dismay we are not adults yet! So this complicated matter should not fall solely on our shoulders; unfortunately, we need help. We need those helpful reminders that, yes, are the bane of our existence. If we took on the entire responsibility with no guidelines, we would most likely run down our bodies in a matter of days.

However, experimenting with sleep teaches us the importance of sleep and our body's needs. I couldn't see, and sometimes still can't see, my mother's point of view if I don't experience exhaustion and the symptoms of sleep deprivation. So maybe teenagers need to learn to deal with the consequences of being exhausted, such as irritability and edginess. The consequences, although drastic, motivate teens to maintain a healthy sleep schedule.

One thing I love about my schedule is that *I* created it. The downfall of my creation is that when I don't get enough sleep it's *my* fault, not my parents'. If I'm tired, I have no one to blame but myself.

So compromising works. Find a certain number of hours of sleep on which you both can agree and then give your kids guidelines and the responsibility for following them. If they do a good job, then great, let them keep on doing it. If they have problems, then yes, it's necessary to intervene.

Q: Do you have any other words of advice for parents about helping their kids get enough sleep?

A: There are a lot of things listed in Chapter 8 that parents can do to help their kids get more sleep. But here are some things that worked for me that parents might want to talk about with their own kids to see if they'll work for their family:

- Like most teens, I have a lot going on in my life, and some of it is hard for my parents to understand. When I lie down at night and try to fall asleep, I have a million thoughts running around in my head: I have a math test the next day, I have to get notes from the history class I missed, I'm going out with some friends on the weekend, is this guy having a party, etc., etc. My secret to clearing my mind is writing down all of my thoughts. I find a scrap piece of paper by the nightstand and get everything out of my mind so I can stop thinking about it. You don't have to write in full sentences—you can just write "party," "notes," "tennis," anything that helps you. If you encourage your kids to write down their worries, their fears, their excitement, their grief, it will help, I promise.

Another Teen Says . . .

❝ Self-discipline is very important in getting enough sleep. Lack of discipline has made my sleep problems worse. ❞

- I got into a routine. At 10:45 I sign off from IMing or hang up the phone, at 11:00 I brush my teeth, at 11:05 I lay out my clothes, at 11:10 I read for 20 minutes, at 11:30 I'm in bed. Of course, this changes a bit sometimes, but it's a pretty usual pattern during the school week. Teens should set up whatever works for them, whatever will help them get good sleep time. The most important part is to enforce the routine every day until it becomes almost automatic.

- I get a lot of exercise, but I try not to exercise within an hour of going to bed.

- At night I try to do some things that will take my mind off school and other stressors. Your student could call a friend, talk online, watch TV, read a book, drink some herb tea—anything to relax the body and the mind.

8

10 "No-War" Ways to Improve Your Teen's Sleep Habits for Optimum Health, Learning, and Living

In the previous chapter you learned a number of ways you can start talking to your teen about getting the right amount and the best quality of sleep—without starting World War III. My daughter Elyssa told you about what worked—and didn't work—for her and how she came to understand that sleep is a priority.

Now I want to tell you about 10 different ways you can help your teen actually get that all-important sleep—without starting World War III. All of the strategies have been field tested with both my patients and my daughters and have proven to be very beneficial in helping them improve their sleep habits.

Before I start talking about the 10 steps, though, I want to emphasize that improving sleep habits needs to be a cooperative effort—you can do everything in your power to convince your teen that she needs to get a reasonable amount of sleep, but you can't *make* her sleep. Achieving good results will happen by calmly (and at a nonstressful time) providing guidelines and suggestions, then encouraging your teen to work out and take ownership of the sleep routine that seems best, then letting her follow the routine—and either reap the benefits or suffer through the consequences. Many parents of teens would love to just lay down the rules and have them followed, but at this age adolescents want to be independent and feel in charge. It may take compro-

Hard as it may be to believe, you're not the only one who freaks out when you look at your teen's topsy-turvy room. Completely cluttered bedrooms actually rattle many of their inhabitants, adding yet more low-level anxiety to their already stressful world. They won't want to clean it up, most likely, but, though it's hard to get them to own up to it, being in there doesn't make them feel good either. Many teens feel happier in a more balanced room, and feel overwhelmed if their room is pretty much a disaster area. Try gently asking your teen if she would like help sorting through things, but keep in mind that teens like to feel their room is their domain—even if it looks like the city dump.

mising on both your parts to find a solution that works, but the rewards will definitely be worth it.

To aid your discussions, you might recommend that your teen read through this book or at least some of the chapters, including this one. Or try leaving the book along your teen's path to the refrigerator—it might just get picked up and browsed.

Strategy 1: Establish a Sleep-Friendly Environment

If your teen's room is a calm, comfy, cozy place to be, it's much more likely that she will be able to relax and, yes, actually sleep there. Try these tips for creating an appealing, sleep-promoting haven:

- Encourage your teen to rearrange the furniture to make her feel comfortable and the room feel different, to reinforce the idea that a change is being made—for the better. You might even propose a trip to a yard sale or favorite store to pick up a few inexpensive items to add a new, personal touch. Or your teen might want to pick out some posters or make a collage of photos, drawings, and memorabilia. Give your teen free rein (within budget restrictions) and encourage creativity to turn the room into a sanctuary that makes her feel soothed, relaxed, and ready to wind down.

COLOR IT CALM

According to color consultants and Feng Shui specialists, soft blues and greens are great colors for bedrooms because they're easy on the eyes and promote relaxation. Other good color choices are beige, tan, light yellow, and peach.

- To make room for the new things and to give the space a less frenetic feel, encourage your teen to get rid of excess belongings. While your daughter probably hates to clean the room, if it's part of a room makeover it's more likely to happen. Offer to lend a hand, but leave the choice of what stays and what goes up to her.

- Talk with your teen about finding a space other than the bedroom to do homework; the bedroom should be a place just for relaxing activities and sleeping. Suggest your teen use the dining room table or any quiet place where there won't be interruptions and she won't hear other family members on the phone or watching TV. Books and papers will have to be put away at the end of the evening, but it's likely work will get done more quickly in a place without distractions.

- Try to keep your teen's room a bit on the cool side at night. Your body prepares you for sleep by lowering your temperature, and a cool room can aid in that process.

Strategy 2: Limit the Use of Tvs, Phones, Instant Messaging, Video Games, and Computers

Staying connected requires that teens stay awake. By limiting plugged-in time, you'll be promoting sleep time. (See how the variety of electronics works to keep your teen from getting enough rest in Chapter 5.)

- Ask your teen to pick a time to say goodnight to friends on the phone or sign off from the computer—after she has finished doing homework, turned off the TV, and gotten ready for bed. Having a set time will keep communication from going on all night, but if it's at the end of the evening teens won't feel they're missing much, since their buddies will need to sleep too.

- If there's a TV in your teen's bedroom, think about moving it out; having a TV in the bedroom is not a teen right of passage. A TV is a big distraction, and it will be easier for your teen to turn it off and move on if it's not in the same place where she sleeps. To encourage teens to watch less TV, remind them that programming is funded by commercials whose goal it is to keep them watching. Urge your kids not to let advertising turn them into an easy mark and to decide for themselves what's cool—with enough rest they'll be more clearheaded and better able to make good decisions. Ask kids to be selective about what they watch and to turn off the TV the moment their program is over—without letting the next commercial play.

•   While watching TV can keep kids up, listening to music can help them sleep. If your teen is in bed and can't sleep, have her plug into a CD or MP3 player with the goal of listening to soothing music to relax and go to sleep by. Remind your teen to choose the music carefully and to keep the volume low and the room lights off. A Case Western University study reported that people who play calm music for 45 minutes before bedtime drift off sooner and sleep longer than those who try to fall asleep in silence.

In addition to MP3 players, stereo systems or boom boxes can provide soothing sounds. CDs of gentle nature sounds, such as waterfalls or waves breaking, can lull listeners to sleep as well as block out any outside noise. You might want to give your teen a gift of a soothing CD you like—she might even try it. A number of years ago I gave my eldest daughter Yanni's *In My Time* and she still uses it to relax and wind down.

•   Like TV, video games can be a way for teens to relax. But like TV, they can also be extraordinarily engaging and problematic. If your teen is an avid game player, encourage her to play the current favorites in the afternoon, as a way to take a break after school is over and before activities, dinner, and homework begin. Also encourage your teen *not* to play video or computer games after 10:00 at night—the excitement of trying to beat the clock or conquer the enemy or make it to the next level can make it hard for teens to stop playing, and the stimulating activity and fast-moving graphics can make it hard to fall asleep when the game is over.

•   As an alternative to playing video games and watching TV, suggest that your teen take up a more calming activity that sparks her interest—something that will still be enjoyable yet soothe the psyche rather than rev it up. The last hour of the day could be spent on a favorite craft or hobby, such as jewelry making, tying flies, or drawing; reading a book or a magazine for pleasure; writing in a diary or journal; playing a quiet online game such as chess or solitaire; listening to music (at a low level); or playing an instrument. My oldest daughter likes to collect thoughtful and insightful sayings and adages and re-write them into a journal. See if there's an activity your teen would like to pursue that will bring a feeling of peace and serenity and help her wind down. It could be the time many teens crave for solitude, privacy, and self-expression.

Strategy 3: Encourage Healthy Eating Habits

What you eat and when you eat it can have a big influence on both your ability to fall asleep and how well you sleep. The following tips will help your teen chalk up a greater amount of high-quality sleep:

- Talk with your teen about the influence food has on sleep. Tell your teen that big meals close to bedtime require digestive processes that can keep her awake. Aid your teen in eating earlier by changing the household dinner hour if necessary; if dinner is usually eaten later than 7:00, work on moving it up. (Eating earlier in the evening will be good for you, too, since you absorb fewer fats from an early meal; that's because, unless you're a complete couch potato, you'll generally do some physical activity after dinner.)

- Encourage your teen to help out with dinner by making a salad or setting the table. Not only will it get her involved with what's eaten, but it may earn her points for something for which she's politicking!

- Talk with your teen about avoiding sleep-preventing caffeinated foods and drinks after 4:00 p.m. This includes chocolate, both as a food group and hot cocoa; green and black teas and, of course, regular coffee; and sodas. Tell your teen that sugar also gives some people a "sugar rush" and keeps them awake.

- Before lights out, drinking a cup of warm herbal tea or warm milk (without the chocolate) can help teens wind down.

- If your teen is trying to lose weight, remind her that skipping dinner is not the solution. If you don't eat dinner, you'll feel hungry all night and your brain will keep you awake to eat. Then not only won't you sleep, but you'll be more likely to eat junk food late at night and take in more calories than you would have if you'd eaten a normal dinner. If your teen is hungry before turning in, advise a light snack of

" I usually snack a little about half an hour before I go to bed. Ice cream is my favorite snack, but most often I have herbal tea, which I find very soothing. If I didn't eat enough for dinner, I can wake up during the night hungry and have to go down to the kitchen for some carbs. That's a hassle, so I try to get enough in before I go to sleep. "

yogurt, trail mix (without chocolate), fruit, cheese and crackers, or a protein power bar. This kind of snack will stave off hunger through the night and is light enough not to interfere with sleep (a heavy snack at bedtime will keep you up as your body digests it).

• Encourage your teen to get to know her body and to avoid eating the foods that will prevent sleep. A trip to the grocery store will help her identify good things to eat and figure out which brands and flavors of foods, including protein bars, are best. Remind your teen to respect her body and to put only good things into it. Junk food is OK occasionally if it's balanced by something healthy.

I usually advise teenage patients and their parents that if they want the ice cream they should have it, but first they should have a turkey sandwich or some form of protein—something low fat that's good for them.

Strategy 4: Establish Successful Bedtime and Wake-Up Routines

The more rested you are, the more capable you are of facing that early-morning alarm, not to mention the rest of the day. To help teens maximize their sleep time and function at their best, take a look at these helpful hints:

• The best sleep comes from following a regular sleep-wake routine. Work with your teen to establish realistic weekday bed and wake-up times that won't vary by more than two hours on the weekends. By getting her input, rather than setting up rules yourself, it's much more likely she'll buy into the plan.

• Talk with your teen about ways to reduce the time she needs to get out the door in the morning so she can get a few more precious minutes of sleep. This can include:

– Showering before bed instead of in the morning

– Making the all-important clothes choices the night before, so there's no need to make decisions (or change her mind three times) in the morning

– Making certain the night before that all the clothes—including socks or stockings and underwear—that are needed are available or will be available; if clothes are in the to-be-washed or to-be-ironed pile, teens can negotiate with their parents to do it for them—or choose something else

– Organizing all accessories ahead of time

– Making lunch together the night before; a list of easy-to-assemble foods your teen likes will help ensure they're in the fridge and make it easy to put something together in a hurry

– Setting all needed books, papers, and homework where they won't be forgotten and can be grabbed easily in the morning

LOSE THE SNOOZE BUTTON

Though many people think that using the snooze button on their alarm clock gives them a few extra minutes of rest, it actually reduces the quality of their sleep. Hitting the snooze button every few minutes just interrupts the sleep cycle again and again, keeping you from waking up feeling refreshed. Setting the alarm for 10 or 15 minutes later than usual and getting right up when it goes off will provide 10 or 15 minutes of additional quality sleep.

• Encourage your teen to think up ways to recognize her achievement when bedtime and morning hassles are kept to a minimum. You can negotiate what will happen or what she will be given as a reward, but do acknowledge the effort when she gets her act together.

• Ask your teen to try keeping a diary in which she writes during the last hour before bed. Writing in a diary has two functions: It helps the winding-down process by providing an outlet for private self-expression and helps the teen feel organized and less stressed about the day ahead.

Teens can use their diaries to write short stories or poetry, about whatever is on their mind, about the guy or girl they're thinking of dating, what ticks them off about someone, how they can talk to a friend about something important, random thoughts, hopes and dreams. They can even write about something they need to get off their chest but don't want to say out loud; adolescents have a lot of drama in their lives but may find some issues hard to talk about. Writing about them instead gives them a way to get it all out. This "flushing to paper," as I call it, is something just for the teen, with no one correcting the grammar and no one saying what's right or wrong.

Teens can also use their diaries in organizational ways, for example, to inventory their day to determine what still needs doing and to think ahead to the following day or days. They can review assignments, work out a schedule, note an upcoming orthodontist appointment or a friend's birthday, and make plans for an upcoming activity. In this way the diary can act as a day planner as well as a creative outlet.

Strategy 5: Control Light Exposure and Brain Cues

Because light signals the brain that it's daytime and therefore time to be up and around, it's critical that teens be exposed to less light in the evening and a lot of light in the morning. To help make this happen:

• After 9:00 p.m., have your teen use a reading light or a clip-on book light to focus light instead of having it come from overhead and all around. Make sure that the bulb is the lowest wattage she can read by without straining her eyes. After 10:00 p.m., when schoolwork is done, have your teen wear sunglasses. Not only do teens think this is cool, but the lower light cues their brain that it's getting darker out and time to wind down.

• Limit TV watching after 10:00 (or after 11:00 depending on your teen's wake-up time), because the TV's strobing lights promote wakefulness. The content is also designed to keep you engaged and prevent you from turning the TV off.

• If a neighbor's outside light shines into your teen's bedroom window, put up a black-out shade to help entrain your teen's brain to the sleep-wake timing that's needed. Or have your teen try using eyeshades (earplugs may help, too, if a lot of noise comes in from outside).

• To help with the morning wake-up process, urge your teen to pull up the shades, turn on the lights in the bathroom, and let the light tell her brain that it's the morning and time to wake up. All the lights don't need to be turned on at the same time—that may be too traumatic—but by the time your teen has been up for 7 to10 minutes all the lights should be on. You might even want to encourage your teen to go outdoors if the sun is out, perhaps to bring in the newspaper or let out the dog.

• Encourage your teen to take some physical steps to aid the wake-up process, including washing her face with cool water and actually running to the kitchen for breakfast. Physical activity in combination with light exposure is a great morning cue to the brain to synchronize its circadian clock with the times *you* have determined are optimal.

> ### A TEEN'S TAKE
>
> **"** *"I follow a regimen. On school nights I always lay out my clothes for the following day, so I can just get up and go. I also try to get up within the same 15- or 20-minute period in the morning. I don't like to use the snooze button because it doesn't go off again for 15 minutes, but sometimes I'll reset the alarm for another five minutes. I also don't like turning on too many lights too fast.* **"**

• If waking up is particularly difficult, your teen might benefit from using a light box or wearing a light visor while getting ready for school in the morning. See the following chapter for more about light aids, where to find them, and how to use them.

Strategy 6: Set Up a Realistic Homework Routine—and Eliminate All-Nighters

One of the most challenging time-management tasks teens face every day is getting their homework done. Here are some tips to help them do it without doing themselves—or their families—in:

• Urge your teen to alternate exercise or break time with study time: work for an hour and then take a 10- to 15-minute break. Shoot some hoops, stretch for a few minutes, check e-mail messages (but then sign off and go back to work), or eat an evening snack. Your teen's brain will work better if it has a few minutes to rest and recuperate.

• With everything they have to do, teens need to plan ahead. If they have a paper due next week, they should outline it this week—staying up writing the whole paper the night before it's due will produce a much poorer product. On the other hand, if they outline a paper and then work on it again a day or two later, their REM sleep will help them organize it and they'll have more and better ideas. An outline will also make the writing go faster and will give students another section to work on if they get hung up on one part.

MAKING A PLAN

A day planner is a great tool for busy, involved teens. Teens can go the low-tech route with a small, inexpensive paper planner—one that can fit easily in a pocket, purse, or backpack and is available in most drugstores, office supply centers, or their school—or take the high-tech route with a PalmPilot or other electronic organizer. After each class teens can write in their assignment, when it's due, and any materials they'll need to complete it. They can also jot down extracurricular particulars if they'd like. For teens, as for many adults, it's hard to think ahead two or three weeks when the current day is completely packed and all-involving. By writing down what's needed and when, they're less likely to wait until the last minute, waste time, or forget what they have to accomplish. Having all their to-dos written down also should reduce stress.

• Encourage your teen not to be fooled by a night with little homework. Putting it off can lead to a really late bedtime, but getting it over with right away will give them a night in which to relax a bit.

• Discuss with your teen how to structure homework time around things she wants to do. If the choice is to watch a particular TV show at 9:00, it's important to get the bulk of the homework done beforehand. If it's to practice lacrosse plays right after dinner, at least one homework project should be done before going outside.

• Urge your teen not to cram for exams or quizzes. For example, instead of waiting to learn all the vocabulary words in one night, she should go over them for a few minutes every night as part of daily studying. This approach will produce much greater comprehension than if your teen waits to learn all the words at once.

• Encourage your teen to do homework in a comfortable spot where there won't be any interruptions by siblings, parents, the phone, or e-mail. Before homework begins, ask your teen to let friends know that she is signing off for an hour or more for homework and won't be available.

• Ask your teen to read the statistics detailed in Chapter 4. They should reinforce your counsel that all-nighters should be a thing of the past. Last-minute studying puts teens at a disadvantage compared to students who give information the sleep time it needs to be incorporated and refined in their brains.

Strategy 7: Reduce Stress

There's no doubt about it—school is exhausting. Not to mention the sports, activities, homework, after-school jobs, family time, and responsibilities that are also part of a teen's day. To help your teen cope with all there is to do, suggest some of the following stress reducers as a way to cope, wind down, and rejuvenate:

• Teens should reward themselves for surviving another school day by doing something relaxing for at least half an hour when they get home. They can nap if they must, but they shouldn't sleep for more than 30 minutes (see more on napping below). Instead, they should try:

– Listening to music or watching TV (they can tape a favorite show that's on at night and watch it after school)

– Eating a delicious—and healthy—snack (a bit of junk food is OK if it's accompanied by something nutritious)

– Getting some exercise if they haven't already had sports

practice—go for a jog, exercise or dance to a tape, take a yoga class, lift weights with a friend

– Showering or taking a warm bath—both are great stress reducers and can keep wound-up teens from tangling with a family member if they start soaking as soon as they get home

– Having a friend come home with them to catch up, watch a program together, or listen to music

• Teens should be careful about calling friends and "ragging" about something or someone. The more they dwell on an issue, the more time they'll waste on it and the more wound up they'll get. Encourage your teen not to call someone up and take her on for something that happened that day. Waiting a day to bring it up will give your teen time and a good night's sleep, which will provide a better perspective on the problem.

• Urge your teen to ask for help to sort out difficult issues. Friends may want to be supportive, but taking a friend's side may not always allow them to give the best advice. A good rule of thumb is that if something bugs you for more than two days, then it's time to find someone outside your usual group to talk with about it. Encourage your teen to pick someone she respects: a parent, relative, minister or rabbi, neighbor, teacher, or therapist.

• Teens will benefit from planning their homework for the week; it's often necessary to start big projects earlier than they think they should. By pacing themselves and distributing their workload throughout the week, they'll do better work and be less stressed. And if a teacher springs another project on them in the middle of the week, they won't get completely crazy but will be able to get it done.

• It's important for teens not to sit around for hours moaning

---

One Teen Says . . .

❝I keep a pen and paper by the side of my bed. If I think of something I need to do the next day while I'm trying to fall asleep, and start worrying that I won't remember it in the morning, I write it down as a reminder. Once I've got it down, it's off my mind. **❞**

about all they have to do; an incredible amount of time can be lost in worrying and complaining. Urge your teen to get in gear and just do it. In fact, encourage her to do the most difficult project first and the easy stuff closest to bedtime. The quality of homework is directly related to how rested teens are when they do it and to whether or not they've done it in a rush. If teens get the rest they need at night, they'll be able to stay focused in class and do their homework much more easily.

- Teens will really benefit by writing in a journal or diary about anything that's worrying them (see page 122 for more about diary writing) and perhaps work on a plan that will resolve the issue. They can also read something soothing or inspiring, such as *Chicken Soup for the Teenage Soul* or some favorite poems.

- Talk with your teen about not taking on too much. There are only so many hours in a day, and some of them need to be unscheduled to have the opportunity to regroup and refresh.

Strategy 8: Restrict Napping

Sometimes sleep-deprived teens are just going to have to take a nap. When that time arrives, encourage your teen to follow these guidelines:

- Teens shouldn't nap for more than 40 minutes (20 or 30 is better). Anything longer may let them cycle into deep slow wave sleep that will make it very hard for them to wake up. When they do wake up, they may actually feel worse than they did before the nap— sluggish, disoriented, and very cranky.

- Teens shouldn't nap late in the day; the later they nap, the harder it will be to fall asleep at night. If your teen knows she is going to need a nap to get through all the homework, the nap should take place as early as possible after school. Any nap should be over no later than 6:00 p.m.

- Teens should set up a mechanism for waking themselves after a short nap. If an alarm clock is too brutal, they should enlist a parent or sibling to get them up. But if they wake up cranky, they need to promise they won't take it out on the person who woke them.

- If possible, it's a great idea to take a brisk walk or do something active to break out of a post-nap fog.

One Teen Says . . .

❝ *I'm often rather pooped when I come home from school, which can vary from 4 to 7. Once I came home from school and was so exhausted that I decided to take a nap. I went up to my bed and fell asleep around 4:30. Well, it was winter and it got dark fairly early. After sleeping like a rock, I woke up in my dark room and saw that it was dark outside. Because I always get up before the sun comes up, when I looked at my clock and saw it was 6:55 I freaked out—my bus comes at 7:05! Feeling like I was having a heart attack, I jumped out of bed and ran down to the kitchen in a panic—and smelled broccoli. Now, my mom has cooked some pretty strange things, but we have never had broccoli for breakfast. After looking around I finally pieced it together. My mom was cooking dinner, and it was 7:00 p.m. My heart kept pounding and I felt like such an idiot.* **❞**

- Teens who feel so tired that they want to nap every day are not getting enough sleep at night and need to adjust their bedtime to get at least another half hour of sleep.
- If possible, teens should substitute a relaxing activity for a nap.

Strategy 9: Increase Exercise

Exercise is not only a great stress reducer; it also keeps you fit, helps you look good, makes you feel good about yourself, and makes it easier to fall asleep. If your teen is not participating in a sport, encourage her to work an exercise routine into two or more days of the week.

- Talk with your teen about an exercise or a sport that she might like. It could be running, using a stationary bike or cycling outdoors, working out on a cross-trainer or with free weights, or any of the following possibilities:
    – Working out to an exercise video—there are videos targeted to both men and women—or to a TV exercise program that was taped
    – Using relatively inexpensive but effective equipment at home, including weights, jump ropes, and chin-up bars

One Teen Says . . .

❝ *My night-owl schedule used to be so bad that I would stay up late, wake up early for school, feel tired all day, then take a nap when I got home. Because of the nap I couldn't fall asleep at a decent hour at night and kept repeating the same thing over and over. The cycle was very hard to break.* **❞**

–– Trading an hour of filing or other work at a local exercise facility for a one-hour exercise class

–– Trying something brand new, such as kick-boxing, yoga, or salsa dancing

–– Working out with a friend following the exercise routine he or she likes to do; it's a great way to get toned as well as have fun

• Encourage your teen to exercise after school or early in the evening. Being physically active too close to bedtime can result in revving you up instead of helping you wind down. However, a few minutes of easy stretching or yoga exercises right before bed can help promote relaxation and sleep.

> **SNOOZE NEWS**
>
> The National Sleep Foundation reminds teens who find it hard to work an exercise routine into their day that they can exercise while doing something else. For example, they can walk on a treadmill while reading or listening to music or do sit-ups and lift free weights while watching TV.

Strategy 10: Recognize and Stop Enabling Poor Sleep Habits

If your teen is falling off the sleepiness scale, a careful evaluation of her schedule will help make the need for sleep more clear. The following suggestions will then help to make more and better sleep a reality:

• Have your teen keep a sleep log—a record of daily bed and wake-up times (see below for the one my patients use)—for a week or two, including at least two weekends. (Research shows that teens ideally need between eight and a half and nine and a half hours of sleep per night, and the log will show how greatly your teen is sleep deprived.) After reviewing the log, have your teen make some lists: one list of the things she likes to do, with a star next to the ones there's no time for; a list of her academic goals, with the time that needs to be spent on each one each week; and a list of personal physical fitness goals (weight loss, amount to be able to press, time to run a mile, etc.). As part of the list making, ask your teen to spend some time thinking about what really makes her happy.

Then have your teen take a careful look at the current sleep-wake schedule and consider her after-school routine. Next, have her start improving the schedule by making adjustments, including:

- Defining a time she will be in bed with the lights out
- Taking the TV out of the bedroom
- Picking a time to sign off the computer and load the CD or MP3 player with her favorite soothing music
- Organizing her homework routine and planning breaks to do some of the things on the list of favorite things to do
- Rewarding herself with some exercise time
- Encouraging you and your spouse to serve dinner earlier and to buy healthy snacks to help control her eating habits
- Personalizing her room so that it promotes relaxation
- Choosing a study nook for doing homework uninterrupted
- Deciding to get more sleep
- Avoiding late-night encounters with parents that might provoke arguments; for example, resolving to ask for permission to go to a concert early in the evening so there's time to work out a solution and cool off if needed before bedtime
- Managing her own sleep-wake schedule to show growing maturity and to keep the peace in the household

Night	6 PM	9 PM	12 M	3 AM	6 AM	9 AM	12 N	3 PM	6 PM	Comments
Monday		T O	●————————————		● C				/\/\/\	exhausted
Tuesday		T O	●————————————		● C				C	tired
Wednesday		T O	●		● C			/\/\/\		tired
Thursday		O	●		● C				C	exhausted
Friday		T	○	●		●		E		OK
Saturday	/\/\/\		○	●		●				pretty good
Sunday			○	●	● C				C	exhausted
Monday			○	●	● C			E	/\/\/\	exhausted

Legend: ○ = in bed   ●—● = asleep   /\/\/\ = nap   C=caffeine   E=exercise   F=food   T=TV   H=homework

Teen sleep log illustrating typical pattern of shortened sleep time during the school week with later bed time and catch-up sleep on weekends.

My sleep log, adapted for adolescents from one designed by Arthur Spielman, Ph.D., a behavioral specialist and coauthor of The Insomnia Answer, can be extremely helpful when you're trying to get a handle on the amount of sleep your teen is really getting. Ask your teen to fill the log out in the morning using the symbols at the bottom of the form; you or your teen can add more symbols if you like—for example, for exercise or drinking caffeinated beverages. An open circle should note the time your teen gets in bed; a closed circle and a line should indicate the time she falls asleep. The line should be broken with a space if your teen wakes up during the night.

9

Getting Off the Night Shift:
Resetting Your Teen's Internal Clock

For many sleepy teens, taking the steps detailed in Chapter 8 will go a long way toward paying down their sleep debt and getting onto a track that will bring them a better quality and a greater amount of sleep. By taking control of their surroundings, their schedule, and how they treat their body, they can reap the benefits of a complete night of energizing sleep.

For teens whose sleep-wake cycles are greatly out of whack, though, some additional steps may be necessary. When adolescent night owls come to see me, I discuss with them the 10 sleep strategies and encourage them to put them in place right away. But we also talk about how the timing of their sleep is delayed and about what it will take to shift that timing to allow them eight and a half to nine and a half hours of nighttime sleep.

Education, then, is an important part of resetting a teen's clock to a more normal, manageable sleep-wake cycle. To make the needed changes, teens have to understand both why they're out of sync and the process for getting back in. But they also have to *want* to make the changes. If they don't think they have a problem or they're happy with the way things are, it will be next to impossible to successfully shift their cycle.

Some kids, particularly younger teens, can be adamant about not wanting to change; then both education and guidance are critical (and a little psychology doesn't hurt). One of my patients, 13-year-old Eric, told me that his mother was "stupid" for bringing him to a doctor and that although his teachers said he was exhausted and falling asleep in class, he was only falling asleep because he was completely bored. Hostility oozed out of every pore, and I knew that laying down a lot of rules on him wasn't going to work. Instead, I asked him if he was able to fall asleep at 9:00 a.m. His answer was a snarly "Sure." Well, I said, most people are well rested at 9:00 in the morning, and if you can fall asleep then, something is wrong—you're not getting enough rest. If you think nothing's wrong, though, why don't you show me? Do a daytime sleep study for me, and after we do it tell me what you think happened and I'll tell you what your brain waves told me happened. If you're not falling asleep quicker than what's normal during the day, then I'll get everyone off your case and you can keep on going just the way you're going.

There was a lot of fast talking on my part, to be sure. But I chose my words carefully to allow Eric to see for himself that something was wrong—and he did. When his sleep study showed that he was falling asleep immediately after being given the opportunity to nap during the day, he began to see that there was a problem—and, after putting up a bit longer with my spiel, that something could be done to make him less drowsy and irritable.

In addition to using a light box and taking melatonin—part of the treatment I typically prescribe and that I'll detail below—I recommended that this patient, who was a little pudgy, start working out with weights and paying attention to his body (I also recommended that he check in with his pediatrician or family doctor, which I always do before having an adolescent patient embark on an exercise program, especially one that involves weights). This encouraged him even more, because the idea of getting buff appealed to him. I wouldn't say he was the most compliant patient I've ever had, but education, evidence, and a little bit of stroking helped him agree to begin treatment—and put effort into adjusting his sleep phase delay.

One Patient Says . . .

❝You need to take the whole problem of changing your schedule head on. Every little thing you do helps. There's no part of the regimen that can be minimized. **❞**

Treating a Resistant Clock

There are four parts to my program for shifting teens' late-to-bed, late-to-rise cycle. Three of the components are therapies—light therapy, melatonin, and chronotherapy; and one is behavioral—having a mature, responsible attitude. While each can provide a great deal of improvement on its own, studies have shown that it takes therapy plus positive behavior to maximize results. You need to apply the complete package.

One point before I begin. You may be wondering why I don't recommend simply taking a sleeping pill to adjust patients' sleep and wake-up times. The answer is: If a teen's circadian clock is programmed to send her to sleep at 2:00 a.m. and wake her up at 10:00 a.m., taking a sleeping pill, or hypnotic, at 10:00 p.m. isn't going to make her fall asleep then and sleep for the next eight hours. Sleep-promoting medication works only when taken during the appropriate "circadian window" for sleep, in sync with where the clock is set for sleep. Hypnotics won't move the clock. Only by shifting a teen's sleep phase will she be able to fall asleep and wake up at more normal hours.

Light Therapy

While much of my discussion so far has been aimed at getting teens to fall asleep earlier at night, it's also critical for them to be able to get up earlier in the morning—both to get to school on time and to start the process that will make them sleepy again at a reasonable hour that night. Many teens set alarm clocks all over their rooms or ask their parents or siblings to drag them out of bed each morning—I even had a patient who asked his mother to throw ice water on him—but there's something more useful, and less jolting, that they can do to help entrain themselves to a more successful pattern.

Light therapy, or bright-light therapy, as it often is called, uses artificial light to help restore the natural circadian rhythm; it's one of the most powerful components of my program. Bright-light therapy provides much brighter light than standard indoor lighting and even more than the outdoor light of a clear spring morning. The reason it's used? The intense light augments and amplifies the natural ambient light that signals the brain that it's morning and time to rise and shine. When the artificial light enters the eye, it travels to the brain and, just as bright outdoor light would do, cues the suprachiasmatic nucleus (if you need a refresher on this process, see page 15) to stimulate the body to wake up.

The ability of bright-light therapy to wake the body up and adjust the sleep-wake cycle depends on several things: the duration of its use, the intensity of the light, the timing of its use, the number of exposures to the light, and the consistency of its use. The spectrum of the wavelengths may also make a difference, and studies are now being done to measure their effects. Blue light appears to have stronger circadian effects than red light.

LUX VERSUS LUMENS

The intensity of bright light is measured in what is called "lux," the international unit of illumination. But lux is not the same as "lumens," which is a measurement of the amount of light at the surface of a light source. Lux is measured at a distance from the light source—the intensity drops off exponentially with distance—which in the case of light boxes and light visors is the distance from the source to your eyes. A minimum of 2,500 lux is required for effective bright-light therapy, and 10,000 lux is generally recommended. To give you an idea of the intensity of that level of light, most home lighting is between 100 and 300 lux and most office lighting is closer to 700 lux.

When I recommend that patients begin bright-light therapy, I usually ask them to do it first thing in the morning for 20 to 30 minutes, or as long as they can before leaving for school; even 15 minutes is better than nothing. Exposure as soon as they wake up reinforces their wake-up time, and bathing themselves in the bright light morning after morning helps to set a pattern. If teens routinely treat themselves with light in this way, they should start seeing clear effects in about six to eight weeks. However, bright-light therapy has immediate alerting effects. Studies show that the light suppresses melatonin and increases activity in attention pathways in the brain. It also has a mild antidepressant effect, especially for seasonal affective disorder, in which sufferers experience a mood disorder during the winter, when there are fewer hours of sunlight.

Currently there are several different products that provide the intense light needed to reset a stubborn clock: light boxes, light visors, and light books. None require a prescription, and all are readily available. (For catalogs or ordering information, contact one of the companies listed in Resources.)

Light Boxes

For quite some time, light boxes were the only source of bright-light therapy, and they are still a very effective way to receive cycle-reinforcing light. A light box, as the name implies, is a fixture that houses a set of lightbulbs. The bulbs are usually white fluorescent or full-color-spectrum bulbs or a tube that's hidden behind a diffuser and tilted forward so the light angles down. The positioning reduces glare while letting more light into the eyes; the diffuser spreads the light out more evenly and absorbs and filters out potentially harmful ultraviolet (UV) rays. Light boxes, which deliver 10,000 lux of light, should be positioned so the light is level with the user's eyes, but it's not necessary to look directly into it. A light box can be placed 14 to 36 inches away from the user; consult the manufacturer's product information to determine optimal placement.

Light boxes can be purchased in several different sizes and intensities. Larger models are available on floor stands so that you can stand in front of them to receive light, for example, while you're walking on a treadmill. Other boxes, some of which look like desk lamps, are smaller and can be placed on a table while you're eating or reading.

Light treatment should be used in the morning as soon after wake-up as possible. The same beneficial effect may be achieved with the use of a light box (left) or a light visor (right).

Still other models are so compact that they can be carried with you when you travel.

ARE THEY SAFE?

Bright-light treatment using professionally constructed light boxes, light visors, or light books is considered to be safe. Extensive studies have shown no damaging effects on the eyes from either short-term (up to 4 weeks) or long-term (3 to 10 years) therapy. However, UV rays can damage the eyes and the skin, so be sure to use a light box that meets the safety standards of the Society for Light Treatment and Biological Rhythms (www.websciences.org/sltbr). That will ensure there is no UV exposure.

Light Visors

Available only recently, lights visors are a practical alternative to light boxes, especially for the rushed adolescent. Worn on the head like a sports visor, light visors are powered by rechargeable batteries

One Teen Says . . .

"I thought wearing a light visor was really weird in the beginning and I thought the light was going to bother my eyes and give me a headache. But the visor is easy to use, and I'm not stuck sitting at the kitchen table with a light box. Most importantly, it's really working and helping me fall asleep earlier. One morning I actually woke up before my alarm! **"**

and project blue-spectrum light down very close to the eyes. While earlier versions of wearable light, which were actually glasses with lights attached, were fairly cumbersome to wear, today's visors are smaller and much more lightweight. A popular visor delivers 8,000 or 12,000 lux (there are two settings) and should be used for 20 to 30 minutes each morning, just like a light box.

Light Books

The size of a small DVD player, approximately $8 \times 8 \times 1\frac{1}{2}$, the light book is the latest light-therapy product. It employs a blue light diode and provides the same amount of lux as a light box but at a lower and, for some, more comfortable intensity. Because of their small size and the fact that you can flip them open and shut, they're easy to use, convenient for travel, and hard to damage.

A NATURAL ALTERNATIVE

If using a light box, visor, or book isn't an option for your teen, although I strongly urge at least trying it before ruling it out, she can still optimize light exposure to reinforce a better sleep pattern. Especially in the summer, your teen can spend early sunny mornings outdoors where the sunshine will help entrain a sleep-wake rhythm. I often recommend that delayed-phase teens take outdoor construction jobs or become camp counselors during the summer to be regularly exposed to bright morning light—as well as rigorous, sleep-promoting work and a regimented schedule.

So how do you choose which product your teen should use? It all depends on her schedule and style. Many of my adolescent patients prefer to wear the visor because they're used to wearing hats or caps and because it frees them from having to sit still in front of a light box or a light book. I ask patients who use a visor to put it on as soon as they dry off from the shower in the morning and to keep it on while they dress, eat breakfast, and get themselves ready for school. Because the visor is mobile, the kids can still rush around as much as they need to while using all the available time to soak up as much light as possible. If you can get them to do it, they could even wear the light visor in the car as they're driven to school (I haven't yet met a teen who was willing to wear a visor on the bus, but I have thought about suggesting that school buses have bright lights inside!).

The light box and the light book, though, are also good alternatives. Although teens need to sit in front of them to receive the light being emitted, and perhaps get up a bit earlier to use either one of them, they could get their light quota while eating breakfast or while going over study notes for an exam. They could also share a large light box treatment with a sibling and have someone to talk to while getting their daily dose.

SIMULATING THE DAWN

Still another light product, for use in the bedroom, is the Dawn Simulator. It mimics a sunrise, gradually increasing the amount of light in the sleeper's room. While it doesn't provide the intense light and therapeutic effect of a light box, light visor, or light book—it provides standard indoor light levels—it does offer a gentle transition to morning.

Will there be any side effects from treatment? Light therapy is thought of as safe and effective, with very few side effects, if any. Headache, nausea, jitteryness, and eye irritation are rare transient side effects that often improve or disappear by the end of the first week of treatment. If they persist, decreasing the intensity of the light by changing the setting, moving the light farther away, shortening exposure time, or avoiding reading during treatment may be helpful. However, individuals with a history of bipolar disease or mania should be especially cautious when using light therapy and have their condition under good control before using it. Anyone taking a drug associated with a photosensitive skin reaction, such as tetracycline, should check with their doctor or pharmacist before starting light therapy, as should patients with eye disease or any chronic condition that might affect the eyes.

Melatonin

In Chapters 1 and 3 I talked about how melatonin, when secreted from the pineal gland, plays an important role in setting our circadian clocks. Taken orally in synthetic pill form—it comes in a range of doses and can be purchased in a drugstore without a prescription—melatonin also helps to reset out-of-sync clocks.

How does it work? Let's say your daughter needs to wake up at 6:30 at the latest to make it to school on time. To get the eight hours of sleep she needs (nine would be wonderful, but we'll take eight), she would need to fall asleep at 10:30 p.m. But her sleep phase delay keeps her from feeling sleepy until midnight. (Remember that melatonin secretion begins approximately 10 hours after wakeup and six hours before sleep.) To help her feel sleepy closer to 10:30, she would take a small amount of melatonin six hours earlier, at around 4:30 or 5:00 in the afternoon, after she gets home from school. By doing this for approximately six to eight weeks, the melatonin would help entrain your daughter to a more comfortable and healthful sleep-wake cycle.

A large dose of the drug isn't needed. When I first started prescribing melatonin 15 years ago, I had patients take it later in the evening and in 3-milligram doses; it was thought to have a hypnotic effect and the recommendation was to take it at bedtime. But it was not particularly effective; studies have now shown that melatonin is

---

One Patient Says . . .

❝Trying to wake up at the same time every day is critical. Otherwise we set ourselves up for failure the next night. ❞

much more of a clock setter than a sleeping pill. So now I prescribe 200 to 500 micrograms (1,000 micrograms = 1 milligram) to be taken about six hours before a bedtime that will provide eight straight hours of sleep.

I don't always prescribe melatonin, though. I only do so if parents are comfortable having their son or daughter take it. But it's not a drug—the Food and Drug Administration classifies it as an herbal preparation that is safe to use. Doses as high as 60 milligrams have produced no major side effects, and only rare and minor side effects of vivid dreams or slight tiredness during the day have been seen. Melatonin won't put an insomniac to sleep, but there is strong evidence of its effectiveness in pushing back the sleep clock. In combination with light therapy in the morning it can help keep your teen's sleep onset from slipping later into the night.

Chronotherapy

Chronotherapy isn't a treatment that I prescribe every day. Though it's drug free and device free, I use it only for the most severe cases and when the patient has several straight days that can be given over completely to the therapy. A holiday period or the summer is a good time to use this treatment, particularly the end of summer when your teen may need to move—quickly—from routinely staying up very late to a schedule that will get her up on time for school.

Chronotherapy actually takes a very different approach from light therapy or taking melatonin. Both of those treatments work to pull the sleep-wake cycle back earlier, say, from falling asleep at 2:00 in the

	Bedtime	Wake-up Time
DAY 1	6:00 A.M.	2:00 P.M.
DAY 2	10:00 A.M.	6:00 P.M.
DAY 3	2:00 P.M.	10:00 P.M.
DAY 4	6:00 P.M.	2:00 A.M.
DAY 5	10:00 P.M.	6:00 A.M.

Chronotherapy: 4-hour phase advancement treatment program.

One Parent Said . . .

❝ *This treatment was a family bonding experience. We worked as a team to help Jason wake up and stay awake when he needed to and to keep things quiet for him when he was supposed to sleep. When it was over, Jason was awed by the fact that he really became able to go to sleep at 10 p.m.—he hadn't thought it was possible.* **❞**

---

morning to feeling sleepy at 11:00 at night. Chronotherapy works with the teen body clock's comfort zone, pushing the sleep-wake cycle later—until it moves around the clock to a more normal time. This is physiologically easier than trying to phase advance to an earlier bed-time.

It works like this. Say your daughter's typical sleep time is 2:00 a.m.—she just doesn't feel tired any earlier. So let her stay up even later—give her a gift she'll love and tell her she should follow her physiological direction and stay up until 6:00 a.m. Every night after that, move her bed-time later by four hours and allow an eight-hour block for sleep. By the fifth night she should be going to bed at a more normal and healthful 10:00 p.m. (I usually use a five-day treatment period, but if more time is available, the process can move forward in two- or three-hour rather than four-hour blocks).

While your teen may feel a bit strange through this process, being awake and asleep at unusual times, there shouldn't be

SNOOZE NEWS

For any of the treatments recommended, it's important to have a structure around which to orient a sleep-wake schedule. During the school year, that's school. During the summer, it can be a job, camp, or specific activities. Without a structure, teens can drift back into staying up too late and sleeping all morning—and become sleep deprived once more and need to phase shift all over again. If your teen's schedule does drift away during a laid-back summer, try to get her back on target as soon as possible—it's disastrous to wait until the week before school begins.

any ill effects and the adjustment takes place very quickly. She will have to stick with the schedule to really entrain it, but falling asleep as soon as she gets in bed should help with its adoption. Taking melatonin to simulate the dim light melatonin onset of the desired schedule, in this case 4:00 p.m., will also keep the schedule from slipping back out in time, as will the critical ingredient of bright light at the 6:00 a.m. wake-up time.

If your teen agrees to try this phase-shifting process, you might · want to suggest that she do it with a friend. While the friend may not be on as late a schedule as your teen, she can be a great support and make the time more enjoyable. It's also a good idea for your teen to have scheduled activities during awake times, to get lots of exercise, and to turn off her cell or bedroom phone during the daytime hours devoted to sleep. A plus for this therapy is that it can be a time for your teen to do things she normally can't, like go to a special spot to watch the sunrise or star gaze very late at night.

Behavior

Whether you and your teen choose to use light therapy and/or melatonin or chronotherapy, an additional key ingredient for success must be added: mature and responsible behavior. A proper attitude is necessary for successfully adjusting a debilitating delayed sleep phase.

That means your teen needs to be mature enough to recognize that sleep deprivation is having a negative effect on her health and well-being. She needs to understand that being exhausted just isn't cool, and be able to say, "I don't like the way I feel. I don't like what's happening to me." Then she needs to agree to the best treatment. She also needs to follow through with recommendations: get more exercise, avoid caffeine, use the light box or light visor and take melatonin if prescribed, wear sunglasses in the evening, maintain a weekend wake-up time that's no more than two hours later than the weekday time, turn off the cell phone or tell friends not to call in the middle of the night, eliminate naps or at least keep them to a minimum—all the things I've talked about that can enable eight to nine hours of sleep within an appropriately timed sleep-wake cycle. Your teen needs to take responsibility for getting the sleep she needs.

That, of course, is going to take education as well as discussion. But without your teen's cooperation, the problem won't get solved. Encourage your teen to take charge of her health, and make it known that you're going to help all you can.

If your teen just won't engage in coming up with a solution, and is chronically sleep deprived and feeling awful, you may need to look for an alternative school that starts later; a school that's more amenable to her phase-delayed life can give your teen the extra sleep time needed to live more successfully. Changing schools may seem extreme, and your teen may object strenuously, but if it's the only way to carve out more sleep time, it's a step you should consider seriously. Discussing a school change with your teen can alert her to the seriousness of the situation and motivate her to engage consciously in the treatment program, send a clear message to her that you care and that you're willing to help—that you're a supporter, not an adversary—and give your teen hope that she *can* feel better. You can also work to get your teen's current school to start later in the morning. (See Chapter 13 for more on this topic.)

Putting It All Together

If your teen's circadian clock is in need of normalizing, you may be ready to put into practice one or more of the treatments I've just described. So I'm going to take you through my typical treatment process—which includes using a light box, taking melatonin, and regulating the weekend wake-up time—so that you can see for yourself how it works. (Chronotherapy is pretty straightforward, but it takes several consecutive days to complete and is used only when time and motivation permit.) By addressing your teen's sleep problems early, with the kind of treatment I recommend, you can avoid getting into an extreme situation that may cause a lot of harm.

A Case History

Carson came to see me during the summer before his junior year in high school. On the small side for his age, he had a history of attention deficit hyperactivity disorder (ADHD), for which he was taking Ritalin, and depression, which had improved since he had transferred a few months earlier to a new school that he enjoyed much more. His pediatrician had referred him to my office because he was having great difficulty falling asleep and greater difficulty waking up in the morning. He often awoke with a headache and also coughed a lot when he first woke up. The headache, like the depression, had abated some since his transfer to the new school.

As I talked with Carson, I learned more about both his sleep issues and his life. He told me that he usually got into bed between 11:00 and midnight on weekdays and between midnight and 1:00 a.m. on weekends and that it generally took him several hours to fall asleep. His new school started at 9:00 a.m., which was great, but because it took him so long to fall asleep he was only getting about five and a half hours of sleep a night. He was very sleepy during the day and napped both on the way to school and on the way home. He was not involved in sports or an exercise program though he did walk a bit during the day.

After talking with Carson, who was eager to understand his problem, and getting his history, I did both a physical exam and a neurological exam. I noted Carson's airway dimensions, the size of his tonsils, his chin and jaw structure, the length of his neck, and the overall appearance of his body, looking for any signs that might suggest underlying sleep apnea (see Chapter 10 for more on this disorder). I also looked for overt signs of depression, which I didn't find. Physically, Carson was in good health.

But with a sleep-wake cycle of 3:00 a.m. to 8:30 a.m., Carson was quite sleep deprived and phase delayed, which resulted in the headaches and exhaustion. His problem was significant and was about to become even worse because he was set to start a summer job that required him to be up at 8:00 a.m.

Before prescribing treatment, I had a long discussion with Carson about sleep phase delay and the impact it was having on his ability to function. We went over the mechanisms that govern the timing of sleep, the concepts of Process C and Process S, and the role Carson's sleep-wake behavior played in his problem. I also told him that his being sleep deprived wasn't his fault. Then I told him, and his mother, who was there for the appointment, that there were behavioral as well as pharmacological treatments that would help.

The regimen I recommended was to aim for a bedtime of 11:45 p.m. and a strictly enforced wake-up time of 7:45 a.m. I asked Carson to get a light visor and to wear it for at least 20 minutes as soon as he woke up to signal his suprachiasmatic nucleus that it was time he should be awake. I also asked him to run the steps in his house first thing in the morning to get his adrenaline flowing, to avoid napping in the afternoon, and to take 500 micrograms of melatonin at about 5:30 or 6:00 p.m. to reprogram his body's dim-light melatonin onset. As part of his evening routine I asked him to wear sunglasses for the last two hours before bedtime and to shower and lay out his clothes for the next day to minimize the time he needed to get out the door in the morning.

I also asked him to spend the last hour before bedtime winding down—not watching television, not talking on his cell phone or IMing on the computer—and writing in a journal to release some thoughts and feelings. I suggested that if he still had trouble falling asleep that he listen to soft music in bed, preferably using a headset, or read using a low-intensity book light. I emphasized the need for him to make every effort to stick to the program, including on weekends. I also told him that if he did well on the regimen, eventually he could have a slightly later wake-up time on weekends, but not more than two hours later than during the week. Finally, I gave him a sleep log form (see page 131) to keep a detailed record of what he did and how it went.

When I saw Carson for his follow-up appointment three weeks later, he had already seen some improvement, though it generally takes six to eight weeks to see significant light therapy and melatonin effects. He had stopped taking naps, aided by the fact that he worked all day, and was falling asleep a little more easily at night. And that, of course, gave him more rest, which was already making him feel better. It had been difficult, he said, not to sleep later on the weekends, but he was trying to keep his weekend wake-up time to around 10:00 a.m. He continued to take his antidepressant medication and felt that it was helping his mood, which was a plus for helping his phase delay. All in all he was making good progress, although he still seemed a bit sluggish. So I recommended that he have a thyroid function study done, a vitamin B12 level taken, a blood count taken, and liver function studies done to make sure that there were no additional complicating metabolic or physical factors. I also coached him again to stay with his program to reentrain his sleep-wake cycle. At his next appointment, I expect to hear great results.

Part III

When to Seek Help from Professionals

10

What Are Sleep Disorders and How Should They Be Treated?

Sometimes, even after they've adjusted their sleep-wake patterns and have put much better sleep habits into practice—and even when they're finally getting eight to nine hours of sleep time—teens can still feel tired and irritable during the day. Their health and performance may also continue to suffer, leaving parents at a loss as to what the problem is and what to do next.

Just like adults, teens can suffer from a sleep disorder other than Delayed Sleep Phase Syndrome (DSPS) that can have very serious consequences. It's estimated that more than 70 million Americans endure one of the many known sleep disorders and that many of these people develop the problem in their teens.

But diagnosis and treatment are often slow in coming. A 1998 study of 548 patients with narcolepsy, the first major national study that provided extensive information about the history of symptoms, revealed that it took patients an average of 15 years from the first complaint of sleepiness to a health care professional until a diagnosis was reached and treatment begun.

The reasons for this? There are several:

• Detailed knowledge of sleep disorders is lacking in the general medical community. For the past 18 years I've been given only one hour of time (this year it's up to an hour and a half) in George Washington University's medical school curriculum to teach medical students about sleep—that's it for their entire four years of medical school. Older docs may not have received any formal training on sleep, since sleep as a specialty wasn't even on the map until the mid-1980s.

•   People who are sleepy are often thought of as lazy. That makes it less likely that they'll complain to their doctor about sleepiness and less likely that their complaint will be taken seriously.

•   The importance of sleep for general health and wellness is just moving into the forefront of medical and societal thinking.

•   The soaring costs of health care have limited the time that doctors spend one on one with their patients as well as increased the probability that patients will change doctors as their health plans change. That makes it less likely that a doctor will get to know a patient well enough to make a more challenging diagnosis.

•   Symptoms of sleep disorders can mimic those of sleep deprivation. Patients may not pursue a diagnosis when they're told that the answer to their problem is to get more sleep.

Diagnosing a teen's sleep disorder can be even more challenging because society believes that sleepiness and sleep-ins are the norm for adolescents. But if your teen's delayed-phase issues have been addressed and she still has trouble falling asleep and is excessively sleepy all day, it's time to look into the possibility of a coexisting or alternative sleep disorder.

Because sleep disorders can be the result of, or be associated with, a number of medical conditions, the best way to begin your sleuthing is to have your teen undergo a general physical checkup. If nothing relevant is found, seeing a therapist or psychiatrist for depression-related or behavior-related symptoms may be called for. An overnight sleep study in a sleep lab may provide critical information about how and when your teen sleeps, and a daytime nap study will show the severity of sleepiness.

While there are many different sleep disorders—85 are recognized by the American Sleep Disorders Association—I'm going to cover the four I see most commonly in teens: sleep apnea, narcolepsy, restless legs syndrome, and insomnia. I'll describe typical symptoms and effects to look for and the best available treatments.

Sleep Apnea

While we don't know exactly how many teens experience sleep apnea, it's estimated that 18 million Americans suffer from its effects. The disorder is characterized by loud disruptive snoring, pauses in breathing, gasping for breath, and excessive daytime sleepiness. It can result in headaches, irritability and/or depression, concentration and memory problems, and frequent nighttime urination as well as the very serious consequences of increased risk of high blood pressure, stroke, heart attack, and, in severe cases, death. In adults it can also have the unhappy result of the bed partner needing to sleep in another room—the loud snoring can cause bunkmates to flee before they develop sleep problems of their own.

IT'S A FACT

The word "apnea" comes from the Greek word "pnea," which means to breathe or breathing. In its English version, with the prefix "a," the word means without or not breathing.

What causes all of this mayhem? When a person suffers from sleep apnea, the airway closes completely during sleep, keeping the necessary amount of oxygen from reaching the lungs, body, and brain. To understand how this happens, let's first take a look at what goes on when we breathe.

We breathe as a result of the activity of pacemaker cells located deep in the brain stem. When it's time for us to breathe in, these cells send signals to the chest wall to expand and to the diaphragm to flatten. These actions cause negative pressure to form within the chest cavity, which results in air being sucked in. When it's time to breathe out, the cells tell the muscles of the chest wall and diaphragm to relax, which results in the air being pushed back out. I like to think of people as living accordions, automatically taking air in and sending it out.

Sometimes, though, we choose to override that autopilot system and take an extra deep breath or hold a breath—to blow up a balloon, to dive into a lake, to torture our parents by seeing if we can hold our breath longer than our sibling, for any number of good or nonsensical reasons. We do have some voluntary control over our respiratory muscles and can clamp down on our chest wall muscles to prevent the breath that our pacemaker cells want us to take.

That's fine for 10 or 15 seconds of a breath hold. Initially the pacemaker cells don't get agitated and neither do you—you have a great time trying to outdo your brother or sister. But if you try to hold your breath much longer, the respiratory centers do get more agitated—they get the message that you didn't take a breath and so start sending urgent signals for you to breathe. You can fight them a little longer if you want, but in the end they win—the brain's respiratory centers, which are extremely powerful, force you to take a breath. (Darn, your sibling gets one up on you.)

Though this is the process that happens in the daytime, it's important for understanding what happens with breathing—and sleep apnea—at night. When you lie down to sleep at night, whether or not you have sleep apnea, your brain stem respiratory centers are set to provide you with nice, deep breaths all night long. The muscles in your airway may relax a bit, the way all your muscles relax when you make the transition to sleep, but basically you're set up to breathe well and easily and keep your brain and body oxygenated.

For people with sleep apnea, though, breathing during sleep does not go well. For reasons scientists don't yet understand, sleep apnea sufferers have excessive relaxation of the muscles of the airway around the level of the pharynx—the part of the airway behind the mouth and the tongue—turning what is usually a smooth-walled tube into an irregularly walled, crinkly, smaller, more lax opening. This condition causes sleep apnea patients' airflow to go from fast, efficient, direct, and quiet to loud and turbulent—air gets caught in the pockets of the airway, causing vibrations in the wall of the pharynx—which we know as snoring.

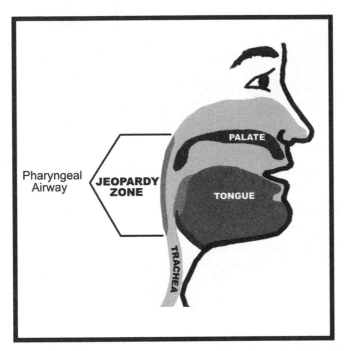

The pharyngeal segment of the airway is lined with muscles that form an open "tube" when the muscles have a good level of tone (resistance) during wakefulness. It is this region of the airway that may relax and close during sleep in individuals with sleep apnea.

IT'S A FACT

Structures in the airway can also contribute to snoring. For example, if you have a long, wide uvula—the small, fleshy appendage that hangs down from the back of your throat—it can lose muscle resistance at night and vibrate in the breeze of breathing. If your tonsils are large, as they can be in kids, they can add to airway irregularity and contribute to snoring as well.

If this is happening to you, things now get really dicey. You're snoring, which is making your bed partner crazy. But beyond that, when you are soundly asleep (in Stage 2), your respiratory centers now signal your chest and diaphragm muscles to take in a bigger pull of

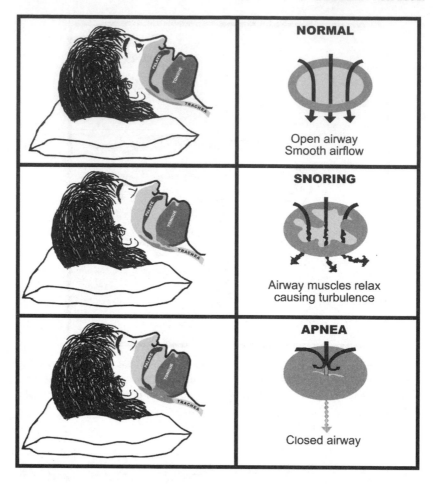

In an individual with sleep apnea there is normal airflow while awake (top). With the onset of drowsiness there is relaxation of the pharyngeal airway resulting in turbulent airflow and snoring (middle). Once asleep, further airway relaxation together with deeper breaths may result in episodic airway closure–sleep apnea (bottom).

air—nice, deep sleep breaths. But as the snoring indicates, your airway is partially closed. So when you draw in air, a vortex develops—a whirling, sucking force that pulls in everything around it—and you suck your own airway shut.

But the respiratory centers don't know this—they think you're breathing because your chest and diaphragm are still moving, trying to pull in air, and they're sending feedback to the brain that they're doing a good job. They don't realize that no air is moving into the lungs. So they signal your muscles to take another deep breath, which causes you to try to pull air through the closed airway—and reinforces the closure. With your airway closed, you get stuck in a blind loop in which you take in no air—an apnea.

A MORE SUBTLE FORM OF SLEEP APNEA

While some teens and children do have flagrant sleep apnea, many others have a more subtle pattern of slight airway closure that results in increased resistance to airflow and an increased rate of arousal. This pattern, called Upper Airway Resistance Syndrome, is considered pathological and can be associated with daytime tiredness. It is more challenging for physicians to make a diagnosis of this condition; a high index of suspicion is necessary.

Luckily, though, your body comes to the rescue. Though your respiratory centers don't recognize that you're not moving air, sensory regions in the major blood vessels that supply blood to the brain—the carotid arteries—realize that the blood passing through them is not fully oxygenated and that carbon dioxide levels may be rising, which means the brain and the body aren't getting the energy they need. Then the carotid arteries activate a reflex mechanism that causes you to partially awaken, though awakenings that accompany apnea events generally are too short to be seen. The awakening, though, increases muscle resistance in the pharyngeal airway and signals the respiratory centers to call for stronger air pulls from the chest wall muscles. This helps to break open the airway and causes you to make a big snorting noise. Airflow is restored—until you drift back to sleep and the whole process starts all over again.

How long does this destructive cycle last? Apnea events typically last 20 seconds but can last longer than a minute—much longer than most people can hold their breath—and they can occur repeatedly all night. Fewer than three events per hour is considered normal in teens and under five per hour in adults, but people with severe sleep apnea have been known to have 60 or even 80 events an hour. That means that not only is their sleep constantly interrupted, making them exhausted and functionally impaired during the day, but also that their health is at greatly increased risk. Waking up to some extent with each apnea event keeps those with the disorder from cycling through all the stages of sleep in sequence and for the proper length of time. Instead, they drift into Stage 1, move into Stage 2, gasp awake to breathe, drift back into Stage 1, move into Stage 2, gasp awake to breathe, over and over again.

Who is most at risk for sleep apnea? While the typical age of onset is 50, and more men are affected than women, teens, especially those with small chin and jaw structures and those who are overweight, also can develop the disorder. Other conditions that put people at risk include:

- A short neck
- A large neck circumference, often 17 inches or greater
- Smoking
- High blood pressure
- Obesity
- A close relative with sleep apnea
- Enlarged tonsils
- Allergies
- Sinus problems
- Asthma

Children with Down syndrome also have increased risk because of small chins, enlarged tonsils, and reduced muscle resistance (hypotonia).

The signs of sleep apnea, as I said earlier, can include significant daytime sleepiness when getting plenty of sleep at night. Snoring is often a key as well, but kids can have sleep apnea without doing a lot of snoring (female adults can also snore less and more quietly). Restless sleep can be an indicator of sleep apnea—the bed covers may be greatly disturbed in the morning—as well as coughing, labored breathing while asleep, acid reflux or heartburn, and many brief awakenings.

During the day, teens with sleep apnea may have little energy and a low mood, but, unlike adults, they may also show their exhaustion in giddiness, hyperactivity, and distractibility. Sometimes teens with sleep apnea are thought to have attention deficit disorder (ADD), because the tiredness is manifested in difficulty with focus, concentration, and attention—key symptoms of ADD, a more common problem in this age group (see Chapter 11).

SNOOZE NEWS

In a recent study of professional football players, 30 percent met the criteria for a diagnosis of sleep apnea. Having a body type that includes a short neck and an increased neck circumference can protect players from neck injuries when they butt heads on the field, but it puts them at risk for obstructive sleep apnea.

Because sleep apnea—and other sleep disorders—may share symptoms of ADD and other more common disorders, it's important for parents to bring concerns about sleep apnea to the attention of their son or daughter's doctor. Many of today's physicians aren't tuned into the possibility of this diagnosis, because tiredness can be associated with the symptoms of several other medical, emotional, and behavioral problems. If you suspect your teen has sleep apnea or another sleep disorder, you may need to become an advocate to make sure she receives help. A sleep study and daytime nap study may be the ultimate diagnostic tools.

A Case History

Chris, a 16-year-old boy, came to see me because he was sleepy all the time and his parents were concerned that he had sleep apnea; Chris's dad had sleep apnea, and they wondered if it could run in families. When I took Chris's history and examined him, I discovered that he had large tonsils but a normal chin position and neck circumference. He wasn't overweight; in fact, he was more on the thin side. His mother told me that he snored a lot, and Chris told me that he played basketball, went to a tough school, had a major academic load, and that he always felt exhausted. He was getting six to seven hours of sleep a night, usually from about midnight to 6:00 or 6:30, and a little more on weekends.

Because of the snoring and the fact that Chris's dad had sleep apnea, my antenna went up and I recommended Chris undergo an overnight sleep study. In addition, I asked him to do a daytime nap study to see exactly how sleepy he was; from his information I knew he was severely sleep deprived. For two weeks before the studies, though, I had Chris regulate his sleep-wake schedule, allocating eight hours for sleep and maintaining a regular pattern. Regulating his schedule in this way would allow us to get an accurate read of his baseline degree of sleepiness.

When Chris did the nap study, it showed that he was profoundly sleepy—he fell asleep in less than five minutes at every nap opportunity we gave him throughout the day. (Well-rested people don't normally sleep at all during nap opportunities.) But the overnight study had even more striking results. It showed that Chris had severe sleep apnea, with 42 apnea events during each hour of sleep—a very surprising finding in a young man without many common risk factors.

Treatment came in three parts. First, I urged Chris to continue to allocate a minimum of eight hours for sleep so that sleep deprivation would not confound his symptoms. Second, because his tonsils were very large, nearly obstructing his airway, I recommended an evaluation by an ear, nose, and throat surgeon. Third, I highly recommended he use a CPAP device (see below) to prevent his airway from closing so that he could have uninterrupted airflow and quality sleep. After protesting quite a bit, because of the way the device would make him look, he decided to use it, and at his first checkup the combination of a longer sleep time and normalized sleep airflow made for a huge improvement. Chris was well rested and felt great. His parents' suspicions had resulted in needed treatment and relief from his symptoms.

If a diagnosis of sleep apnea is made, there are several forms of treatment available. For teens with large tonsils like Chris, a trip to an ear, nose, and throat doctor may result in a tonsillectomy, which can do a great deal to open up the airway. Kids with allergies can use a topical nasal spray or decongestant to ease blocked passages and improve airflow. Overweight teens can help manage their apnea by going on a weight loss and exercise program and keeping the weight off permanently. A dental appliance, in which the top and bottom plates are hinged together, also helps by moving the lower jaw and tongue for-

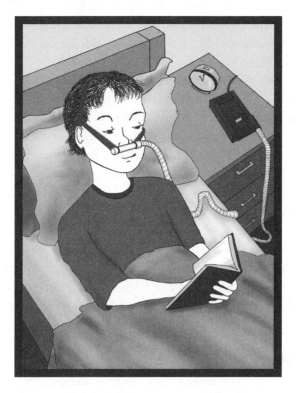

CPAP treatment may be delivered by a small mask covering the nose or a nasal pillow system that seals against the nostrils and connects via tubing to a small air compressor unit at the bedside. The pressure of the inspired air acts like a splint and holds the airway open, which normalizes airflow.

ward to make more space for the airway. If teens have a very small or receding chin or a chin or jaw malformation, surgery to realign the jaw, though a major undertaking with risks, can bring substantial relief. For teens with Upper Airway Resistance Syndrome, any of the above recommendations may help as well as a noninvasive procedure, such as a laser-assisted uvolopalatectomy or injection snoreplasty, to trim the uvula and soft palette.

The most effective, and least risky treatment, however, is for patients to use a CPAP, or Continuous Positive Airway Pressure, device while they sleep. The device, which consists of a mask that fits over the nose or plugs that fit into the nostrils and an air compressor attached to the mask with a hose, pressurizes the air that users breathe in. The increased pressure acts like a splint and holds the airways open, preventing collapse.

Though it's cumbersome to be hooked up to and takes some getting used to, the CPAP device is more than 95 percent effective in preventing apnea events. If adolescents feel weird wearing the mask—or if adults feel self-conscious in front of their bed partner—I always remind them that no one cares what you look like when you sleep, especially if you can be pleasant, energetic, and upbeat the next day.

That said, however, no adolescent on the planet wants to sleep with a CPAP device. So we usually make every effort to use alternate means to treat sleep apnea in teens. However, some teens, like Chris, have such a severe case and such severe symptoms that CPAP is warranted. It helped him enormously, as did having his enlarged tonsils removed several months after I saw him. In fact, the improvements in both the sleep apnea and the daytime sleepiness were so dramatic that Chris was able to stop using the CPAP device.

Narcolepsy

Narcolepsy is a chronic sleep disorder that affects 1 in 2,000 people. The disorder impairs the brain's ability to maintain a normal, sustained awake period—patients have overall sleepiness and may experience sudden sleep attacks at times when they should be awake. They also may experience cataplexy, a condition brought on by strong emotion in which muscle resistance is either abruptly weakened or extinguished and the person wobbles or falls to the floor. Other symptoms can include vivid dreams, or hypnogogic hallucinations, while making the transition into or out of sleep, and the normal paralysis of REM sleep persisting into wakefulness—a frightening condition in which you're awake but can't move. People who have narcolepsy generally sleep an appropriate number of hours at night but still feel sleepy during the day.

While the reason behind the disorder isn't fully understood, a genetic theory and an immunological theory have both been proposed. Recent studies indicate that the disorder is associated with a lack of hypocretin, a brain neurotransmitter that's found in the sleep-

One Patient Says . . .

❝ *Before I was treated, all I did was think about sleep. I rearranged my schedule so I could sleep. On the weekends I never wanted to go anywhere because I knew I had a finite amount of energy and when it was gone I would have to nap. I was always planning how I could sleep and when I could sleep and where I could sleep. But I never talked to people about the problem because I was embarrassed by it and because people misinterpreted my sleepiness as laziness. Plus I come from a family of workaholics, and I always thought fatigue and sleepiness came from overworking and overachieving. It never occurred to me I could have a disease.*

❝ *Now that I've been treated, I keep to a strict sleep regimen. And it's so wonderful to wake up feeling refreshed and not think that it's a tragedy that my sleep is over. I don't have to have my entire life revolve around sleep any longer.* **❞**

---

regulating region of the hypothalamus and the brain stem. Researchers believe that hypocretin is critical for promoting and maintaining wakefulness during the day.

Narcolepsy can affect both men and women and can develop at any age—I've treated patients as young as 6 and as old as 82. However, the peak age of onset is during the teens and early 20s, so narcolepsy should certainly be considered during an evaluation of excessive teen sleepiness. If left untreated, it can significantly impair all aspects of a patient's daily life. Patients who weren't diagnosed until their 30s or later often say that their sleepiness kept them from achieving both their academic and social potential.

What would make you suspect narcolepsy? Sleepiness alone can be a very difficult symptom to evaluate in a teen because there are so many reasons for teens to be sleepy. Certainly evidence of cataplexy would be diagnostic, but episodes of reduced muscle tone may not be an issue for young people at all and adults often have fairly subtle signs of cataplexy because they subliminally blunt their emotions to avoid the extremes that cause severe weakness. Classic cataplexy is seen when a narcoleptic person laughs at a very funny joke and crumples to the floor. But such an obvious manifestation is rare. A much more typical manifestation was evidenced in a patient of mine. Each time she was called to her rather stern boss's office, she'd get halfway through her doorway and her knees would start to buckle—she'd have to stop and regroup.

Subtle evidence of cataplexy can also show up as a weakness in the shoulders or jaw. After laughing for a few seconds, your jaw muscle might get tired and you might not be able to laugh any longer, or your head might sag for a moment. Headaches are also a red flag for possible narcolepsy. Continuing and extreme sleepiness is also something to watch out for, though as I've said sleepiness is symptomatic of many sleep-related issues. As with other sleep disorders, you'll need to first determine if there are underlying physical or emotional causes for your teen's sleepiness, aggressively treat any elements of DSPS, have your teen catch up from any accumulated sleep debt, and then have her do a sleep study and a daytime nap study.

IT'S A FACT

A family history of narcolepsy should also raise the possibility of narcolepsy in your sleepy teen if she doesn't improve after increasing total sleep time and adjusting the sleep-wake schedule.

If narcolepsy is the diagnosis, what are the possible treatments? The first step is to make sure your teen is getting at least the minimum number of hours of nighttime sleep; even though that sleep doesn't relieve sleepiness, it's needed for energy to get through the day. Naps can be helpful, too, though teens should keep them to no more than 20 to 30 minutes and finish them before 6:00 p.m.; they can help teens feel refreshed for the three to four hours following.

Treatment can include the use of wakefulness-promoting drugs such as Modafinil, a nonamphetamine-based compound that improves alertness by supporting the brain's sleep-wake switch and increasing hypocretin. Other standard medications include long- and short-acting methylphenidate derivatives and dextroamphetamine derivatives. Cataplexy in teens is rarely severe enough to require treatment wth drugs.

If your teen needs to take one of the stimulant medications, you may need to speak to her school administrator if she needs to receive a midday dose at school. You or your teen may also need to educate teachers and friends about the possible occurrence of cataplexy if your teen exhibits it.

Restless Legs Syndrome

There's not a lot known about restless legs syndrome (RLS) in kids, though a fair number of adults who have it say that their symptoms first appeared in late childhood or adolescence. But the disorder can make those who have it very uncomfortable. It's characterized by an overwhelming urge to move your limbs, especially your legs, usually beginning at bedtime when you're lying quietly waiting for sleep. You get a creepy, crawly sensation in the calves of your legs—some of my patients call it a building tension—that ends in the urgent need to move them. You also might make a jerky movement with your feet or sometimes a stretching movement. Moving relieves the uncomfortable feeling—many patients resort to pacing—but tension begins to build again almost immediately, ending in another movement in as little as 20 seconds.

Because RLS symptoms often occur when you're ready to sleep, they can impair your ability to relax and transition into sleep. The symptoms may also continue as periodic limb movements while you sleep, causing microarousals during sleep and resulting in daytime sleepiness. Patients who have severe RLS may have symptoms earlier in the evening or even during the daytime when sitting quietly, which can make it torture to read, go to the movies, or drive for a long time.

What causes RLS? Unfortunately, the precise mechanism isn't known. However, Chris Early, a neurologist and sleep expert at Johns Hopkins, recently observed a relationship between RLS and low and low-normal serum iron levels (iron is a critical element of pathways involved in controlling and executing movement). Dr. Early has also observed an improvement in some patients when body iron stores were replenished. Other studies have found a relationship between RLS and diseases of the peripheral nerves and spinal cord, kidney failure, dialysis, pregnancy, Parkinson's disease and other neurodegenerative conditions, and alcoholism. RLS can also occur as a side effect of some medications, particularly SSRIs, or selective serotonin reuptake inhibitors, which are prescribed for depression. Researchers from Stanford University's School of Medicine have reported that about half of the 10 to 15 percent of the population who suffer from RLS have a family member with a history of the disorder, providing evidence that they inherited it.

IT'S A FACT

If you have RLS, the National Sleep Foundation warns that your symptoms can become more severe if you consume caffeine or take antidepressants.

While a diagnosis of RLS in kids is made very infrequently, if your teen is excessively tired and you've seen involuntary movements or your teen has complained of discomfort in her legs or arms and the need to move them, be sure to mention the symptoms to your daughter's doctor. A history of building discomfort in the limbs that is relieved by movement helps distinguish a sleepy teen with DSPS from one with RLS. The doctor should see if an underlying condition exists—iron levels should definitely be checked—or if any medication the teen is taking precipitated or is aggravating the condition (a trial of a lower dose, a dose taken earlier in the day, or an alternative medication may be in order). You don't want to neglect the problem when relief is available.

That relief may come in the form of different kinds of behavioral interventions, such as gentle stretches or yoga exercises in the evening. Some patients have reported that a warm bath or shower can be beneficial. Adult patients may get relief by drinking a glass of quinine water, but I know of no information about the chronic use of quinine water in teens. Boosting potassium stores with orange juice or a banana in the evening also may have some effect, though most likely it won't improve full-blown RLS symptoms.

Sometimes, though we prefer to avoid it with teens, successful treatment requires the use of medication. Drugs that increase brain dopamine, gamma-amino-butyric acid, opioids, and newer-generation anticonvulsants may relieve symptoms. I use anticonvulsants for teens whose symptoms are severe enough to warrant intervention (there is precedent for using these drugs with teens for seizures). There is no increased risk to RLS patients of having any of the disorders, such as Parkinson's disease and epilepsy, that these drugs are usually used to treat.

Insomnia

Though RLS is found infrequently in teens, the sleep disorder insomnia is much more prevalent. According to a report presented at the Associated Professional Sleep Societies' annual meeting, one-third of the 1,014 teenagers who were interviewed for a study said they had had symptoms of insomnia at some point in their lives. A full 94 percent of those teens experienced insomnia symptoms at least twice a week for a month or longer, and 17 percent had full-blown insomnia that "caused noticeable distress and impaired their normal functioning."

I think of insomnia as a symptom of a group of disorders rather than one disease. That's because insomnia encompasses three different sleep problems:

- Trouble falling asleep at night
- Multiple awakenings during the night
- Waking up too early in the morning

For teens the most common problem is falling asleep at night, but they also experience insomnia's other difficulties.

When patients, especially teens, come to see me because they're tired and are having trouble falling asleep, it can be difficult to sort out whether they have a delayed sleep phase or true sleep-onset insomnia. That makes it very important to take a careful history, because stress, anxiety, and lack of a wind-down period in the evening can manifest in insomnia—they're the most common causes of insomnia in teens. While some people respond to stress with stomachaches and by over-eating—I get a crick in my neck—many people find that stress greatly disturbs their ability to fall asleep. They lie in bed and worry and either can't fall asleep or wake up later in the night when they don't want to.

When anxiety and stress dissipate, however, as the problem gets solved, most people move on and return to a regular sleep pattern after just a few sleep-restricted nights. But for other, more susceptible people, the stress-induced insomnia becomes a terrible pattern. Though the stressor goes away, these people continue to associate their bed, where they laid awake worrying, as a place to continue to lie awake and worry—and not sleep. Like Pavlov's dog, who learned to salivate at the ring of a bell that accompanied food—a conditioned response—they become conditioned to getting into bed and having trouble falling asleep. This form of insomnia is called chronic psycho-physiological insomnia.

To help figure out whether a teen has insomnia or a shifted circa-dian rhythm, it's very helpful to know what time she wakes up. While late sleep-ins are the hallmark of DSPS, a teen with insomnia tends to feel tired during the day but wakes up at an appropriate time in the morning. And unlike kids with a delayed sleep phase, teens with in-somnia are usually not impossible to wake up.

It's also important to find out what teens are doing at night. Can they not fall asleep because they just watched a violent TV show? Did they stay up very late talking to a friend? Did they eat a huge snack or exercise just before getting in bed? Are they worrying about some-thing or maybe showing signs of depression? If stress or anxiety ap-pears to be what's keeping your teen awake, the first thing to do is to encourage your teen to talk about what's bothering her with you, a trusted friend, teacher, or counselor. Many problems are tough for teens to solve on their own.

There are also several behavioral therapies that teens can use to keep stress from ruining their sleep. One is to stay out of bed until they're truly tired enough to sleep. Keeping a sleep log will help iden-tify when your teen actually falls asleep, and then she can wait until approximately that time to get into bed. (If it gets too late, resulting in not enough sleep time, your teen can slowly move bedtime earlier after getting into a pattern of falling asleep more easily.) You can also suggest that your teen make some changes to make being in bed a different experience; this will help break the association between being in bed and not sleeping. Rearranging the bedroom, changing rooms with a sibling, or sleeping with their feet at the head of the bed are all ways to create a more positive sleep experience.

Stretching before bed is also a great way to de-stress. Teens can use the routine I recommend (see below) or develop their own set of easy stretches to help them wind down. As I suggested in Chapter 8, teens can also flush to paper: make lists of things that are bugging them, describe troublesome events to help them see another perspective, express wishes or dreams. Listing things they need to do can help them feel more organized and less anxious.

A great tool for getting your mind off your worries is called guided imagery. The idea is to picture a place and an experience you love and relive it—in multisensory, technicolor detail—in order to keep your mind focused on something pleasant and relaxing rather than on something worrisome or stress inducing. Since I love the beach, I relive the sights and sounds of the shore: waking up in a different bed, listening to the sounds of the apartment, going out on the balcony and looking at the early runners on the beach, listening to the ocean, feeling the sun. Then I recall typical beach day events: walking to the bagel shop for breakfast supplies, making sandwiches—who's helping and what we're making—packing the cooler with beach-specific junk food. I also recall the texture of the damp sand on the aluminum frame of the lawn

---

One Teen Says . . .

❝ *When I can't fall asleep because I'm stressing about something, I close my eyes and picture a big stop sign. I use the sign to stop myself from going over and over my problem. Then I replace the sign with something relaxing or pretty, like some candles or the lake where I go.* **❞**

Bedtime Upper Body Weight Routine

Stand at bedside, knees slightly bent. Perform each exercise 12 times
very slowly, gently stretching neck and shoulder girdle musculature.
Begin with comfortable light weights, just enough to offer gentle resistance.

Biceps Curls: Hold
weights palms up
and flex elbows.

Triceps Curls: Hold
weights palms down
and flex elbows.

Upward Rows: Hold
weights palms down
and raise in midline.

Chicken Wings:
Hold weights at
shoulder level
elbows out and
push back.

Push Backs: Hold
weights palms back
at sides and push back.

Shoulder Shrug: Hold
weights at sides and
raise shoulders.

Gentle upper body stretching routine to relax muscles before bedtime.

chairs when I pick them up and stepping out of the building into the sun and the heat. I reach into my memory bank and remember every possible detail. It's a great way to relax and enjoy a positive experience all over again.

Solving the problem of insomnia manifested as multiple wake-ups is a little more difficult, because when you're asleep, of course, you can't use behavioral remedies. The first thing to do is to make sure there are no external causes of the problem, such as the room being too hot, having eaten a late dinner, noise from elsewhere in the household, or having a pet in the bed. Then a careful history should be taken, looking for signs of health-related conditions, such as sleep apnea, RLS, heartburn, or continuing effects from daytime medications, that could be the cause. Since depression is strongly linked to multiple unwanted awakenings, it's also important to rule it out.

While behavioral strategies are extremely effective for managing sleep-onset insomnia, and should be the first line of treatment, they may be less effective for treating multiple nighttime and early morning awakenings. Sleep studies may be needed to evaluate for nocturnal sleep disorders. At times medication may be a reasonable source of relief for these problems, especially extended release hypnotics and selected antidepressants and anticonvulsants. Care needs to be taken, however, when selecting the appropriate drug: Some of these medications promote wakefulness. You'll need to work with your teen's doctor to discover which drug provides relief but, very importantly, you should also continue to use behavioral interventions to minimize prescription drug use.

> **SNOOZE NEWS**
>
> Major life stressors can also be a cause of multiple and early morning wake-ups. The worries of the day can disrupt sleep between 2:00 and 5:00 a.m—3:00 is a particularly fragile time for sleep—and it can be particularly difficult to fall soundly back to sleep afterward. Weeks of early morning awakenings and insufficient sleep time are signals that help is needed. Screening for depression and anxiety disorders, and treating them, is critical.

11

Handling Serious Problems That Can Accompany Lack of Sleep

In the previous chapter I talked about how the symptoms and effects of sleep deprivation can sometimes mask very serious sleep disorders, including sleep apnea and narcolepsy. Being the insidious condition that it is, sleep deprivation sometimes also has symptoms in common with serious physical and mental diseases—and may be both a cause and an effect of them and occur at the same time.

This chapter looks at several of those diseases and provides information that can help in understanding their link to sleep deprivation. Because they can all significantly affect your teen's health and well-being, it's important to keep them in mind when you're trying to uncover why your adolescent is so exhausted—and trying to turn that around. If you suspect your teen might have a serious medical problem, seek out the evaluation and treatment skills of a qualified health care professional.

Thyroid Disease

The thyroid gland is located at the base of the neck in front of the trachea, or windpipe. The gland makes, stores, and releases two hormones: T4, or thyroxine, and T3, or triiodothyronine. These hormones control the rate at which your body's various organs work, what's known as your metabolism. If your thyroid doesn't produce and put enough hormone into your bloodstream, you have what is called hypothyroidism, and your metabolism slows down. If your thyroid makes too much hormone, you develop hyperthyroidism and your metabolism revs up too much. Both of these conditions can seriously impair your health by keeping your body from functioning as it should.

ADDITIONAL SYMPTOMS OF HYPOTHYROIDISM AND HYPERTHYROIDISM

Hypothyroidism:
- Decreased appetite
- Change in menstrual periods
- Feeling cold when others don't
- Constipation
- Muscle aches
- Brittle nails
- Hair loss

Hyperthyroidism:
- Rapid heart beat
- Weight loss
- Increased sweating
- Feeling hot when others don't
- Changes in menstrual periods
- More frequent bowel movements
- Tremors

While the two disorders have different causes, both have symptoms in common with sleep deprivation. Hypothyroidism can cause fatigue, weight gain, decreased energy, and puffiness around the eyes, and hyperthyroidism can produce tiredness, nervousness, and difficulty initiating and sustaining sleep. Though either condition can develop at any age, thyroid disease commonly appears in the teens and early twenties, particularly in women, so it's important to consider it when you have a tired teen evaluated. Some forms of thyroid disease are thought to be genetic, so it's also important to consider it if you have family members with thyroid problems.

To make sure your teen's thyroid is functioning as it should, the doctor will do a blood test as part of a physical checkup. If thyroid disease is discovered, treatment is readily available and effective: supplemental hormones to increase thyroid hormone production or medication to suppress an overactive thyroid gland.

Obesity

In other sections of the book I talk about how sleep deprivation can result in weight gain and obesity, but I'm going to mention it again here because it's so critically important. Childhood obesity has reached epidemic proportions, not only in the United States but in many other countries around the world. It's particularly damaging because it not only negatively affects childhood health and well-being but it can lead to a lifetime of increased health risks and problems, including hypertension and diabetes. Not only that, but obese children who grow up to be obese adults can then be a factor in their own children becoming obese. A recent study in Japan concluded that parental obesity, in addition to long hours of TV watching and physical inactivity, was significantly associated with childhood obesity.

The same study also showed that there is a dose relationship between short sleeping hours and childhood obesity—in other words, the less sleep you get, the more likely you are to become obese in childhood. Late bedtime was also found to be closely related to childhood obesity. The study considered anything less than eight hours of sleep each night as short sleeping time.

Lack of sleep is thought to promote obesity by interfering with the feedback-control pathways between the body and the brain that regulate hunger and appetite. It results in a significant reduction in the secretion of leptin, the hormone that signals the brain to suppress appetite so that we'll stop eating (for more about leptin, see Chapter 2). This in turn results in increased hunger. One study showed a 24 percent increase in hunger that was made even worse by being directed at high-carbohydrate, calorie-filled sweets and starches. Sleep deprivation also promotes obesity because it's a stressor; the body responds to stress by increasing the activity of the autonomic nervous system, which results in elevated levels of the hormone cortisol, which may increase appetite.

Adding to the problem is the fact that when teens are tired they're probably not motivated to exercise and when they're overweight they're not likely to exercise either. But exercise is key to bringing weight down into the normal range, along with eating a nutritional, balanced diet and caring about your body. If your teen is overweight or obese, encourage her to find an exercise program that's fun, and help out by providing encouragement and a fridge stocked with fruits and vegetables. A trip to a nutritionist can provide valuable information on healthy eating.

ANOTHER STUDY REPORTS . . .

The five risks for childhood obesity are:

- Parental obesity
- The child's temperament
- Low parental concern about the child's thinness
- Persistent tantrums by the child over food
- Less sleep time

Diabetes

Diabetes is a disease in which the body doesn't produce or correctly use (resists) insulin, the hormone that's needed to convert sugar, starch, and other foods into energy. The American Diabetes Association estimates that 18.2 million people in the United States currently have diabetes, but that 5.2 million don't realize they do. Kids and adults who have diabetes can suffer serious health problems, such as high blood pressure and abnormal cholesterol, which are associated with a dramatic increase in the risk for heart disease and stroke.

While the causes of diabetes are not fully known, obesity is a major risk factor. A family history can also contribute to it and immune system problems can trigger it. It is also known now that people who have sleep apnea are at an increased risk for insulin resistance and metabolic syndrome, which includes a group of metabolic risk factors, and that studies of sleep deprivation reveal impaired metabolism of sugar.

If there's a history of diabetes in your family or your teen is obese, is sleep deprivation a major additional risk factor for the disease? Research in adults based on the Sleep Heart Health Study, which was funded by the National Heart, Lung, and Blood Institute, reported that, when compared to participants who slept seven to eight hours a night, the risk of diabetes was two and a half times higher for those who slept five hours or less, one and a half times higher for those who slept six hours, and close to two times higher for those who slept nine hours or more—high risks for both short and long sleepers. In addition, sleep deprivation can make it much more difficult to control blood sugar if you have diabetes.

Determining if your sleepy teen has diabetes may be challenging, however, because the two have symptoms in common, including increased fatigue and irritability. Other symptoms of diabetes include frequent urination, excessive thirst, extreme hunger, unusual and unexpected weight loss, and blurry vision.

If you think it's possible that your teen has diabetes or prediabetes, a fasting plasma glucose test or an oral glucose tolerance test in your doctor's office will tell you. As with many health issues, following a balanced diet and getting plenty of exercise, along with doctor-prescribed medication, will go far in managing the disease. The report on the research mentioned above also suggests that getting the right amount of rest may be a successful addition to the treatment plan for people with reduced glucose tolerance and diabetes.

Headaches

Frequent, bothersome headaches are a ubiquitous complaint among the teenagers I see who have Delayed Sleep Phase Syndrome (DSPS). And, right along with issues about sleep, they're also one of the most commonly reported complaints in clinical practice among people of all ages, according to a report by the University of Copenhagen's Department of Neurophysiology. Headaches and sleep problems often go

SNOOZE NEWS

In a study done through the National Hospital for Nervous Diseases in London and reported in the journal *Cephalalgia*, 25 healthy subjects who experienced one to three hours of sleep loss for one to three nights suffered subsequent headaches that lasted from one hour to all day.

hand in hand, so if your teen is exhausted and has frequent headaches, she may have a significant sleep delay, sleep deficit, or sleep disturbance.

What causes these headaches? The precise mechanism isn't known yet, but there is evidence that both sleep deprivation and sleepiness itself, whatever its cause, may be associated with an increase in headaches. A study by the Scripps Clinic noted that changes in sleep duration and sleep quality seem to affect headaches of different types and the University of Copenhagen study mentioned above reported that sleep fragmentation and insomnia were both related to headaches.

Headaches typically associated with sleep deprivation and sleepiness include tension headaches characterized by a tight bandlike sensation and heaviness that may begin in the morning and build as the day goes on. Pain is often greatest over the temples and the forehead. Migraines, those painful, throbbing headaches that can be accompanied by vomiting or vision disturbances, may also occur more frequently and more intensely in the sleep deprived. A study carried out at Case Western Reserve University found evidence that children who get migraines also have frequent sleep disturbances.

Cluster headaches, a variant of migraines that often occur during the night, also may be brought on or aggravated by sleep loss and stress. Altered melatonin levels have been seen in cluster and migraine headaches, making treatment of headaches with melatonin a potential area for future investigation.

If a phase delay or a sleep disturbance is resulting in headaches that are making your teen miserable, treating the sleep issue is a must.

One Teen Says . . .

" *I get morning tension headaches whenever I'm severely sleep deprived. Because of them I get to school late a lot and I feel really sick most of the morning.* "

In my practice teens with headaches severe enough to keep them out of school often and who haven't responded to multiple medications have seen significant improvement in headache frequency and intensity when their total sleep time is lengthened and their circadian disturbance treated.

A study reported in the journal *Seminars in Neurology* noted that headaches not secondary to a sleep disturbance also can be eased by addressing sleep issues.

Impaired Immune System

Will you really get sick if you don't get a good night's sleep? Probably not, if it's just one night. But chronic sleep debt is a different story. With long-term sleep deprivation your body loses some of its ability to fight infection.

One of the ways our immune system protects us from disease is by scavenging up free radicals, the atoms formed as byproducts of metabolic activity that can damage our tissues by reacting with our cells or cell membranes. Under healthy conditions, antioxidants are sent by the immune system to end free-radical chain reactions before they can damage vital cells and cause disease. With as little as 5 or 10 days of sleep deprivation, however, one study showed that many different antioxidants decreased in major organs to levels that are associated with impaired health. The data suggested that levels of antioxidants diminish with sleep deprivation and that sleep deprivation is therefore a risk factor for disease, which can include everything from frequent infections to cancer.

Frequent infections are something I see regularly in my exhausted teenage patients with sleep phase delay—they seem to catch everything. And not only do they catch everything, but it takes them a long time to get healthy again; they come in coughing and three weeks later when I see them for a follow-up they're still coughing. Sleep deprivation can not only contribute to catching infections but can aggravate existing ones, prolonging recovery.

Detailed experiments based on animal models of sleep deprivation have documented a clear relationship between the immune system and sleep. Carol Everson, a prominent researcher, has led many

❝Sleep deprivation never helps anyone get over a cold and can actually be one of the main factors in contracting a cold or the flu. I know that if I start feeling sniffly or sneezy I have to get extra sleep that night to fight it off. When you feel achy from a cold coming on and you're sleep deprived, it's an uncomfortable disaster. ❞

studies involving lab rats that point out how prolonged sleep deprivation clearly disrupts immune function. One study, known as the Table-Over-Water sleep deprivation model, is a case in point. In the study, rats walked on a table that turned over a pool of water. The table had a section missing, and if the rats didn't keep walking they would fall into the opening, drop into the water, and drown.

Because rats have a great survival instinct, the rats in the study kept walking and walking. They were given all the food and water they wanted, but they didn't sleep. Soon they developed a hypothalamus dysfunction syndrome that resulted in weight loss despite overeating, hair loss, and skin lesions. And then they died—every rat that was sleep deprived for 10 days or longer eventually died. Without suffering a cut or having another source of infection, and despite the activation of their immune response, they died from infection caused by the breakdown of the immune barrier in the gastrointestinal tract. The normal bacteria of the GI tract became pathogenic.

IT'S A FACT

Though the immune system can fail because of sleep deprivation, the first reaction is actually for it to rev up, a process called upregulation. This appears to be a protective process, almost as though the immune system knows it's going to have a problem providing immunity when the body and brain don't get enough sleep. Unfortunately, though, upregulation may not completely compensate for sleep loss. When you're in a sleep-deprived state, as many teenagers constantly are, infection wins.

There is good news here, though, along with all the bad. With sleep, your body can fight harder against infection and even reverse its damaging effects. In the study in which many rats died from constantly walking and not sleeping, other rats were rescued from the water table and allowed to sleep. The skinny, hairless, exhausted creatures revived and returned to normal health with no other treatment. When rats get 80 percent of the sleep they require they do not contract fatal infections and they do survive.

Seizure Disorders

Approximately 1 percent of the population will be diagnosed with epilepsy by the age of 20. The disorder is characterized by recurring seizures that can be associated with loss of consciousness as they begin, jerking movements of the limbs often accompanied by tongue biting or loss of bladder control, and a period of unresponsiveness when the seizure ends. Because two-thirds of those who experience epilepsy first experience it in childhood, many teens around the world must cope with this debilitating condition as they're coping with adolescence.

There are many different forms of seizures. Absence seizures (formally called petit mal seizures) may be associated with a brief interruption of consciousness, sometimes accompanied by staring or rhythmic blinking; and complex partial seizures, experienced as alterations of consciousness in which there can be intrusive thoughts, a sense of disconnection, or a sense of déjà vu accompanied by chewing or fumbling movements. There are also seizures that begin with twitching or sensory disturbances in the face or limbs and then either stop or go on to cause a generalized seizure.

What is the connection between seizure disorders and sleep loss or sleep disorders? The risk of having a seizure is greatest during both the transition into or out of sleep as well as during sleep, and it is well established that sleep deprivation and disorders that interfere with the quantity or quality of sleep can increase seizure frequency. Teens with known seizure disorders are at great risk of loss of seizure control when they're sleep deprived because of DSPS. Sleep deprivation may also be a triggering factor in teens who are at risk for seizures because of a history of serious head trauma or a strong family history of seizures—some types of seizures have an increased genetic risk.

At times, distinguishing between subtle seizure disorders and sleep-related phenomena can be challenging. For example, the brief staring spells of absence seizures may look very similar to microsleeps. The chewing or fumbling often seen in complex partial seizures can also be seen during sleep attacks. So if you've witnessed unusual behavior in your teen, I recommend that you take her for a consultation with your doctor or a neurologist. Diagnosing a seizure disorder requires taking a careful history and an electroencephalogram (EEG) to monitor brain wave activity and sometimes repeated monitoring and clinical observation.

If a seizure disorder is the diagnosis, treatment will likely be an anticonvulsant drug. It's also critical for your teen to avoid sleep deprivation.

VERY CLOSE TO HOME

The similarities between sleep disorders and seizure disorders became all too clear to me recently when my 17-year-old patient Brenda slumped in her waiting-room chair and began making chewing motions. When my staff and I rushed out to her, she was hard to wake up and her muscles were limp. As we carried her back to my sleep lab, she came around somewhat but then fell back into the altered state. Quickly we hooked her up to monitoring electrodes to observe her brain wave activity—and were very surprised. Her brain wave pattern showed her to be in REM sleep—she wasn't having a seizure.

Fifteen minutes later, Brenda woke up on her own and told me that she remembered hearing my staff and me talking in the waiting room. A complete workup of Brenda revealed a history of severe sleepiness. There was also evidence of sleep attacks and some weakness episodes brought on by emotion, which were suggestive of cataplexy. I made the diagnosis of narcolepsy, but without EEG monitoring it might have been hard to do.

Attention Deficit Disorder and Attention Deficit Hyperactivity Disorder

If a careful sleep history isn't taken during an office visit, a sleep-deprived child or adolescent may be misdiagnosed with attention deficit disorder, or ADD, often because the key symptoms of ADD—having difficulty focusing, paying attention, and concentrating—are also key symptoms of sleepiness and sleep deprivation. Kids are also more likely than adults to show evidence of sleepiness in restlessness and distractibility, further confusing sleep deprivation with ADD. Kids with ADD have also been shown to have more nighttime awakenings and arousals, more movement during the night, and poorer quality sleep.

ADHD BEHAVIORS

According to the *Diagnostic and Statistical Manual of Mental Disorders*, three patterns of behavior may indicate ADHD:

- Being consistently inattentive
- Being consistently hyperactive and impulsive
- Being consistently inattentive, hyperactive, and impulsive

Symptoms often appear over the course of several months, with impulsiveness and hyperactivity often noticeable before inattention. The symptoms are not consistent with the child's developmental level and some may have been present before the age of 7. The behaviors of the condition can make it hard to function well in social, academic, and work-related activities.

Just what is ADD? The disorder is a condition in which kids have trouble paying attention and concentrating. It can be seen without hyperactivity in quiet, distractible kids and with hyperactivity in kids who are also distractible (with hyperactivity the condition is known as attention deficit hyperactivity disorder, or ADHD, but I'm going to use ADD here for both forms of the disorder). The distractibility can cause kids to get into trouble at school, so the condition may be accompanied by behavioral issues. It's estimated that between 3 and 5 percent of children have ADD, approximately 2 million children in the United

States. The causes of the disorder aren't fully understood, but it appears that genetics and biology may be involved and that environmental factors may contribute to the severity.

When teenagers come to my office, it's not unusual for me to learn that they've already been diagnosed with ADD (though I don't entertain that diagnosis until the patient's sleep schedule has been regulated and all the aspects of DSPS have been treated). Sometimes it makes me wonder which is the chicken and which is the egg: Do kids with ADD have trouble paying attention because they don't sleep as well as other kids, or do kids who don't sleep well develop serious problems with attention? Many researchers are also interested in that question, and the link between sleep deprivation and ADD is now under scrutiny.

In a study of that link by M. K. le Bourgeois and colleagues at the Bradley Hospital Sleep and Chronobiology Research Laboratory at Brown Medical School, reported in the journal *Sleep*, subjects with all types of ADD had poorer quality sleep as well as greater daytime sleepiness than control subjects. Children with ADD have also been found to have more frequent periodic limb movements during sleep, which can fragment sleep and further aggravate daytime alertness and attention.

Because ADD and sleep deprivation share so much turf, making an accurate diagnosis can be extremely hard. Your teen's physician or a specialist can help in the determination, but be sure your teen's sleep-wake schedule is regulated and that she is well rested before the evaluation takes place.

If ADD is the diagnosis, it's likely the doctor will prescribe a stimulant drug to help with attentiveness. But if your teen has a sleep phase delay and/or is sleep deprived, that condition needs to be taken into account. Stimulant drugs taken during the day can spill over into the nighttime, disturbing sleep and making your teen even more sleep deprived. So it's important that any medication your teen receives doesn't relieve one problem while contributing to another. It's important to ensure that sleep isn't disturbed.

IT'S A FACT

Research reported by the National Sleep Foundation relays the good news that in many cases people who have ADD and are sleep deprived show great improvement in both conditions when they get enough rest.

Drug and Alcohol Abuse

In a recent report, the American Academy of Sleep Medicine identified symptoms or a history of drug or alcohol abuse as problems that can accompany sleep difficulties. While drinking too much or taking drugs may seem like a strange bedfellow for sleep deprivation, the decrease in emotional control that too little sleep can bring on can lead to out-of-control behavior. Judgment, too, can be impaired by sleep loss, adding fuel to the fire for engaging in destructive and dangerous behaviors.

A report in the journal *Drug and Alcohol Dependency* describing a study performed at the Henry Ford Health Sciences Center agreed that insomnia significantly predicted the onset of substance abuse in adolescents. The use of cigarettes, alcohol, and illicit drugs was associated with adolescents' reports of having frequent sleep problems. While part of the association was attributed to psychiatric problems, such as depression and anxiety, a clear relationship between sleep problems and the use of illicit drugs was shown.

When evaluating a teen with a delayed sleep phase, drug use and drug abuse should be considered as possible complicating factors, especially if the teen shows persistent hostility, failure to comply with treatment, or failure to respond to treatment. A urine drug screen may be helpful in determining if recreational drug use is involved.

Depression

Like ADD and sleep deprivation, depression and sleep deprivation often go hand in hand. Research, and my own experience, tell us that:

- Sleep deprivation increases the risk of depression.
- Sleep debt often increases the severity of depression.

SIGNS OF DEPRESSION

The National Sleep Foundation lists these symptoms as possible signs of depression, which affects about one out of 12 teenagers before the age of 18. Many of these symptoms are also symptoms of sleep deprivation.

•   Feeling persistently sad, hopeless, or empty for several weeks, months, or longer
•   Sleeping more or less than usual
•   Loss of interest in favorite activities
•   Lack of energy
•   Weight changes and appetite disturbances
•   Moodiness
•   Feeling guilty, helpless, or worthless
•   Having difficulty concentrating, remembering things, and making decisions
•   Withdrawing from friends and family
•   Loss of self-esteem and self-confidence
•   Irritability and restlessness
•   Frequent headaches and stomachaches
•   Doing poorly in school
•   Having thoughts of death or suicide

•   Fourteen percent of insomniacs have major depression.
•   Depressed children and adolescents exhibit disturbed sleep continuity.
•   Some forms of depression are associated with increased sleepiness and lack of energy; some agitated forms of depressions are associated with a high level of difficulty initiating sleep and maintaining sleep.
•   The persistence of sleep disturbances increases the risk of recurrent depression.
•   Waking up regularly at 3:00 a.m. is a classic sign of depression.
•   Sleep deprivation and depression can both interfere with the ability to think clearly, perform everyday activities, feel well, and enjoy life to the fullest.

Because of these links, and because they can occur simultaneously, it can be extremely difficult to know if an exhausted teen is actually a

One Patient Reports . . .

❝ *I've had problems with sleep my entire life. But going to college was my undoing. My already precarious sleep became wracked by all-nighters as well as drinking and procrastinating. I managed to keep my academic performance together for my freshman year, but my sleep problems kept getting worse. I wasn't able to sleep at night, I slept late into the day and missed classes, and my mood was terrible. I became more and more depressed. The depression and the sleep problem became a vicious cycle.*

❝ *It took failing out of school to wake me up to the idea that something was actually wrong with me, that I needed help. But the maze of professionals I saw—psychologists, psychiatrists, therapists, psychopharmacologists—only made me feel worse. No one knew what was wrong. But some of the doctors told me that when my depression was better the sleep would come around.*

❝ *It seems almost ironic that the last doctor I saw was Dr. Emsellem, but making the decision to go there was the turning point for me. Finally I got a diagnosis—Delayed Sleep Phase Syndrome—that made sense to me, and the medication I took and using a light box had a good effect. Even though things are still far from perfect, it was addressing my sleep problems that allowed me to start living again. I don't know if the sleep problems caused the depression or the other way around, but it was fixing sleep that got me out of that blackly depressed nightmare.* ❞

---

depressed teen—or both. In my practice I see a lot of kids who are both sleepy and depressed; sometimes they've been referred to me by a psychiatrist who's treating them for depression and sometimes I see them and ask them to see a psychiatrist as well. As a sleep doctor I don't treat teens for depression, but if I suspect it's a concurrent condition or a product of sleep issues, I'll refer them so that both problems can be attended to.

A RESEARCH SURPRISE

One unexpected finding, reported by researchers at the National Institutes of Health in the late 1970s, is that in patients with very severe depression, complete sleep deprivation can have an antidepressant effect. However, that effect disappears with just a few minutes—not a few hours—of sleep. And, of course, going without any sleep is not a viable long-term treatment option.

If determining the cause of your teen's tiredness, drop in grades, irritability, and disgust with the world is difficult, helping her get more sleep is a great first step. As long as there's no clear-cut, deep-seeded depression, fixing the sleep problem often fixes any low-grade accompanying depression. But if your teen's mood is truly disturbed and negative, especially if there's a history of depression in your family, it's best to consult a psychiatrist or psychologist. Talking to a therapist can help teens sort through their issues, and an antidepressant, if prescribed, may be very beneficial in conjunction with strategies to treat a delayed sleep phase.

One of those strategies, light therapy (see Chapter 9 for more on this), has been found to improve both mild and moderate depression as well as treat an abnormal circadian rhythm. The Committee on Chronotherapeutics, assembled by the International Society for Affective Disorders, reported that light therapy also is effective for major depression and is a viable treatment for those who can't or won't take medication.

Suicidal Tendencies

According to the National Sleep Foundation, half of all teenagers who go untreated for depression may attempt suicide. The risk of suicide begins to increase during adolescence, and it's the third leading cause of death among teens.

What's the connection between sleep deprivation and suicide? Suicidal patients often report trouble sleeping, particularly because of insomnia, nightmares, and sleep panic attacks. One reason for this link may be the hormone serotonin, according to an article in *Annals of*

Clinical Psychiatry by R. K. Singareddy and R. Balon. The article notes that serotonin plays an important role in initiating and maintaining both slow wave and REM sleep and that it has been found to be low in patients who either attempted or committed suicide.

Adolescents who took part in a sleep study in China gave proof of the association between sleep deprivation and suicidal tendencies. More than 19 percent of the 1,363 students interviewed said they had thought about suicide and more than 10 percent had actually attempted suicide in the previous six months. This is shocking enough, but what is even more shocking is that the average amount of sleep for these students was 7.6 hours a night, not five or six. The conclusion the study drew was that anything less than eight hours of nighttime sleep is associated with an increased risk of suicide.

Thoughts of suicide as well as depression are significant problems on college campuses. In a recent survey taken by the National College Health Assessment program, 61.5 percent of students "felt hopeless at least once per school year," 44 percent "felt so depressed it was difficult to function," and 9.5 percent "seriously considered suicide." A 2002 study put the number of campus suicides at 1,088, and an earlier study showed that the suicide rate among young people had tripled between 1952 and 1997. While substance abuse, anxiety, and feelings of desperation increase the risk, mental illness, usually depression, is the cause of 95 percent of college suicides. Research by Roseanne Armitage at the University of Michigan found that increased sleep problems and increasing reports of depression on college campuses were definitely connected. An article in the Lehigh University student newspaper stated that the average amount of sleep students who were polled had gotten the night before was 5.8 hours.

To treat the major causes of depression and to prevent suicide, professional help is certainly needed. Parents, schools, community resources, and friends also can be important parts of the support system for clinically depressed or suicidal teens. As the above and other studies found, however, getting enough sleep may also reduce the risk of adolescent suicide.

WATCHING OUT FOR ANXIETY

Anxiety disorders and sleep problems have also been found to be linked. Anxiety can aggravate and exacerbate difficulty falling asleep, particularly in teens with a delayed sleep phase. If your teen has significant, regular trouble initiating sleep, it's important to consider the possibility of anxiety and to have her evaluated and treated, if necessary.

Part IV

Family and Community Support

12

Supporting Your Teen

When teenage patients come to my sleep center, they usually come with a parent. Most parents want to be part of the office visit both to hear what I have to say but also to tell me what's going on at home. This, very often, includes the aggravation they're having with their teens from trying to get them out of bed in the morning, battles they're having over getting homework done at anything like a reasonable hour, struggles they're going through trying to cope with grumpy, exhausted noncommunicators, and conflicts over bedtimes and falling grades. Most parents are concerned about what's happening to their tired teens, but they're not sure what the problems really are and don't know how to solve them. That can lead to high-decibel control wars—and very unhappy kids and parents.

Occasionally those control wars break out in my office. When I'm trying to gather information, the adolescent gives her view—sometimes slumped in the chair, grunting out a couple of words—and the parent provides his or her perspective—which the patient then contradicts and the parent repeats, well, let's just say more firmly. This can go on and on until things get so heated that I have to call a timeout in order to sort out the facts and get everyone focused on working on the problems.

One Patient Says . . .

❝ *When you're a teenager, everything your parents say or do sounds like they're yelling at you. It's not necessarily that their voices are raised—at least not in the beginning. It's just that everything they say feels like they're trying to change you. As a teenager you want to be independent. You don't want anyone telling you what to do.* ❞

Parent-teen teamwork is key to helping adolescents get more and better sleep. While it's ultimately the adolescent who has to deal with the results of the biological changes that are affecting her body, parents need to play a supporting role in helping that effort take place. Supporting—not fighting. Supporting—not micromanaging. We all need to understand that it's impossible to make teens sleep just because we want them to or by trying to dictate their every move. It is possible, though, to make it more likely they'll get the sleep they need by taking the following steps.

Take the Problem Seriously

As you now know, sleep deprivation is a serious problem—so it needs to be taken seriously. Though we all wish it were otherwise, it's a problem that affects most teens and one that affects every aspect of their being. In a review of a number of studies on sleep deprivation, G. G. Alvarez and N. T. Ayas of the University of British Columbia and Vancouver General Hospital stated that "A healthy amount of sleep is paramount to leading a healthy and productive lifestyle" and that less than seven hours of sleep a night puts people "at an increased risk of all-cause mortality." The researchers concluded that "sleep should not be considered a luxury."

The first step, then, to ending the sleep wars and helping your teen get more rest is to make sleep a priority for both your teen and your family, including younger children (getting them into good habits now can prevent problems later). Parents need to realize that their teen's exhaustion and health and mood issues are not the result of a "bad stage" that she is going through and that the problem won't go away

One Parent Says . . .

❝ *Parents need to come to grips with the fact that not getting enough sleep is really a problem. It's not a figment of your imagination and it's not a figment of your child's. You can waste years thinking that your child is just going to snap out of it, but they don't do that. As soon as you face up to the fact it makes a huge difference.* ❞

unless both they and their teen do something about it. The parents of patients I see say, without exception, that once they understood the problem and took it seriously, their kids started to do much better. So, parents, we need to wake up to our teens' sleepiness. A huge 71 percent of parents of adolescents, according to the National Sleep Foundation's 2006 Sleep in America poll, believe that their teen gets enough sleep every school night or almost every school night.

Talk to Your Teen

Communicating with your teen is critical as you work together to improve sleep habits. Begin by discussing all the changes of adolescence as well as the importance of sleep; you can use this book as a guide and suggest that your teen reads at least a few parts of it. Then keep talking as your teen develops a sleep program, works at making changes, has successes and failures, and reaps the benefits of sufficient sleep. While that's going on, guide, support, and encourage without taking over—your teen needs to lead the charge and you need to step back into the role of first lieutenant.

Establish the Ground Rules

A close friend of mine used to spend his mornings trying to roust his teenage daughter out of bed for school. He would get up, use the bathroom, and then pound on his daughter's door and yell, "Time to get up, Maria." Then he'd head back to the bathroom and shave, and then pound on his daughter's door again and yell again, "Time to get up, Maria." And then he would get dressed and—you get the picture. Every morning before he left for work he made repeated attempts to get

Maria out of bed—and ended up angry and stressed when he finally faced an equally angry and stressed daughter before they both flew out the door.

My friend called this mode of operation "integrated nagging." I call it unconstructive, unpleasant, and unnecessary.

I speak from experience. As I said in the introduction, my husband and I used to be continually on Elyssa's case to get her out the door in the morning. It's a terrible way for both parents and students to greet each day.

A much better way to handle the start of the day, and other times that can erupt into harsh words, is to agree with your teen ahead of time on how you're going to get through such times more calmly. As you talk about the changes that need to be made and as your teen develops a sleep program, set up some rules of engagement for keeping things under control: both what will happen in each circumstance— what the teen will do and what you and your spouse will do—and what is acceptable behavior.

When I talk with teens and their parents during the first office visit, I challenge them to go home and *quietly* discuss what needs to be done and how they're going to do it. For example, if getting their teen up and out in the morning has been an ongoing source of contention for them, I ask that the teen and the parents find a better way to handle it. I recommend that the family have this talk in the evening when the teen is awake, at her best, and perhaps even apologetic for obnoxious morning behavior.

In Maria and her dad Louis's case, instead of banging on Maria's door every five minutes and yelling, Louis could tell Maria that he'll knock on her door twice but no more—and that she still has to get to school on time. She could say that she won't yell at him when he tries to wake her (she often yelled things she didn't mean, and it was hard for him not to be offended) and that she'll be responsible for getting to school on time. They both could agree not to hold a grudge against each other if the morning doesn't go well.

Figure out what your rules are going to be; drawing up a written contract is very helpful. Will you agree to knock on your teen's door twice and then not anymore? Or would your teen prefer that you come into the room and actually give her a little shake? Does your teen want you to back off completely and let her handle her sleep and wake-up times on her own? If your teen knows she can't get up on her own, will she commit to not yelling at you if you agree to wake her up? (This may be very difficult for your teen, because teens roused from deep slow wave or REM sleep may be barely conscious and not remember later what they said; taping them when they wake up may give you credibility in the negotiations.) If late-night TV watching is a problem, will you both agree that your teen will lose her driving privileges for a week if she stays up until midnight watching? Both of you need to talk about your areas of contention and then clearly define what you're both willing to commit to, what you won't take (you don't need to take any verbal abuse from your teen), and what will happen if things go awry. Then you've got to stick to your plan—which may take some biting of the tongue on your part. For example, if your teen stays up late watching television, you have to keep yourself from getting out of bed and going downstairs to admonish her to go to sleep. Instead, you have to calmly ask for her car key the next morning if no driving privileges was the agreed-upon consequence. If you think you'll be tempted to make a nasty comment at some point, you might want to write down ahead of time the straightforward, unantagonistic words you'll say. If things go well, you might also want to have a list at the ready of positive things you can say or have a reward system in place.

One last point here: Sometimes it turns out that one parent is better able to deal with all the sleep issues than the other, so that person should be the one to take them on. For example, if you're a very meticulous, very structured, very organized kind of person, a teen who straggles out in the morning at the last possible second looking a little

---

Another Parent Says . . .

❝ *Talking over all the sore points and writing up an agreement ended all the pulling and pushing we were going through. I found I had to distance myself sometimes, which was hard, but I learned that that was much better than interfering too much because that just made Matt angry and rebellious.* **❞**

❝ *Once we made the agreement, spelling everything out, I didn't need to interfere. Alicia got herself up in the mornings, wore her light visor, and remembered to take her melatonin in the late afternoon. She's managing her sleep problems and is pretty proud of herself. I'm thrilled to find out that she's mature enough to handle everything on her own. I'm especially glad because she'll be a good role model for my younger child Jake, who's already starting to have a lot of trouble waking up in time for middle school.* **❞**

---

less than pulled together may drive you batty, even if she's actually fulfilling her part of the bargain. But if your spouse doesn't get as upset, it may be best if he or she is the one to work with your teen. Sit down with your spouse and discuss if one or both of you will oversee the agreement. (If neither of you can deal with waking your teen up in the morning, you can arrange to use a wake-up service like Awake123 [www.wake123.com], MyCalls [www.mycalls.net], or Wakeupland [www.wakeupland.com] or ask someone who's not as likely to get screamed at, like a grandparent, to do the honors. Or buy an incredibly loud alarm clock.)

Don't Be an Enabler

Sticking to your agreement can take more than biting your tongue. It may also require that you change some of your habits. That's because, without even realizing it, many of us are enabling our adolescents' bad sleep habits and taking on ourselves the responsibility that should be theirs.

My good friend Joan is a case in point. Every morning for months, Joan had driven her 14-year-old son Ira and her 16-year-old daughter Sarah to school because they couldn't get themselves out of bed in time to make the school bus. Joan would call them and call them to get up, but they never would. Then, at the last minute, they'd drag themselves out but the bus would already have come. So, in her bathrobe, Joan ended up driving them to school every day. The whole thing was infuriating and making her a wreck.

When I heard this story, I counseled Joan that she needed to make an immediate change; her kids had shifted the responsibility for getting to school on time—which was theirs—onto her all-too-accepting shoulders. But before she did she needed to sit down with her kids and tell them what was going to happen. In a calm voice, she needed to say that she wasn't going to drive them to school anymore, that they had alarm clocks, food in the kitchen, and a bus at their disposal and that they needed to make use of them. She also needed to tell them that if they missed the bus they would still have to get themselves to school on time, which would mean they would have to walk.

Joan agreed. She knew it was the right thing to do and that she had to stop enabling her kids' lack of responsibility. But she worried that her kids might suffer if they missed the bus again and she had to follow through. It was two miles from their home to school. And it was in the middle of winter, with temperatures in the 30s. I told her that walking a few miles would be great exercise for her kids, and if she worried they'd be cold she should suggest they wear gloves and hats.

That night, Joan sat down with her kids. Without yelling or getting angry, she told them that from then on she expected them to take the bus to school every morning. She said she would no longer be available to drive them. If they missed the bus because they were late getting up, they would have to get to school on their own.

Well, the next morning came, and guess what? Her kids rolled out of bed at the last minute as usual and asked her to drive them to school "just one more time." But Joan held the line. She told them she wasn't going to drive them, as she had warned, and recommended they wear gloves and hats for the walk to school.

Her kids couldn't believe it. They yelled, they pleaded, they told her she was a terrible mother for making her children walk to school in such cold weather. Her son, the major manipulator, even threatened to call Child Protective Services. Both kids were still protesting when they finally bundled up, slammed out the door, and headed down the driveway.

But they walked. And they made it to school (Joan called the school to make sure). And from then on they woke up in time to take the bus; Joan never had to drive them to school again. By holding firm she stopped playing her children's game and started to receive their respect.

TAKING A POSITIVE APPROACH

It's important not to be an enabler, but it's also important not to take on sleep issues like a vendetta. The agreement you make with your teen does need to be enforced, but you don't want it to be the cause of another war. If things don't go well, it's not necessary to rant and rave; the consequences that were established should simply go into effect. And if things do go well, some positive, reinforcing words will go far. You can even set up a reward system if you want.

Whenever you can, it's also a good idea to give your teen the benefit of the doubt. For example, if your agreement says she'll wear the light visor for 20 minutes every morning, let her try going without it in the summer when she feels she gets more outdoor light and has less trouble waking up.

For a lot of teens, especially those who have often had the way smoothed for them, it can be hard to take on sleep-related responsibilities. But teens really need to understand that they're plenty old enough to take on the job of regulating their sleep-wake schedule and for being a responsible family member. As parents we should support them, but it's not up to us to shoulder the entire load. We don't need to try to wake them 20 times in the morning, we don't need to stay up late putting together a school lunch the night before, we don't need to wake up from our own sleep to make sure they didn't fall asleep in front of the TV. If we do, we're just enabling the continuation of their bad sleep habits and keeping our teens from growing up. A reality check of the dynamics in your household will help you see if some changes need to be made.

Work to Change School Start Times

One of the best ways you can support your teen is to join with other parents and local advocacy groups to have the schools in your area start later in the morning. The extra sleep teens would get would provide a wealth of health benefits, plus schools that have made the change report across-the-board learning improvement. For details on how you can help support this very important effort, see Chapter 13.

Set a Good Example

You know that old expression "The apple doesn't fall far from the tree"? As you work with your teen to increase the amount of sleep she gets and to make improvements in all sleep-related parts of your teen's life, it's extremely important that you model good sleep habits yourself. Your teen might seem to pay absolutely no attention to you, and to care even less about what you're doing, but, believe me, most teens watch carefully what their parents do—sometimes to jump on them, of course, but sometimes to learn, and mimic, the way things should be done.

I bet your teen is no exception. So here are some pointers for being the best influence you can be on your teen's effort to get more and better sleep. And there's a bonus here: If you follow them, not only will you be a supportive, caring parent, but you'll be helping yourself get a better night's sleep too.

Watch Your Night-Owl Behavior

If you tend to stay up late most nights, watching TV, working, or just catching up on the things you didn't get done during the day, your teen may think that it's not that important for her to get to sleep by 11:00. Adults do need less sleep than adolescents, but we still should aim on getting eight hours (at the very least seven hours) and getting to sleep around 11:00 ourselves. Try giving yourself an earlier curfew, and think about turning the tables and asking your teen to help you out. When I say good-night to Elyssa, she says, "Good-night, *Mom,*" in a way that means "You, too."

Watch Your Own TV Watching

I've talked a lot already about how bad an influence I think TV is on teens' ability to fall asleep. Well, it's not good for adults either. Many adults have a TV in their bedroom and can get caught up watching emotion-provoking shows before sleep or turn on the news for a few minutes and end up involved in a two-hour movie. TV watching from bed can be great if you do it for just a short time, mainly to relax. But you might relax even more by following a quiet wind-down routine (see below). If you do want to watch TV before bed and your kids complain that they should be able to as well, let them know that, although you watch a bit, you're already organized for the next day and always able to get to work on time.

Wind Down Before Bed

As it is for your teen, it's a great idea to spend the last hour or so before bed disconnecting from the stresses of the day and getting relaxed before going to sleep. If you watch TV, keep the sound low and look for something nonviolent. Better yet, listen to music, read, or do some light stretching (see a suggested routine on page 170) or yoga. A household wind-down time will help everyone sleep better—and get along better too.

Keep Caffeine and Alcohol to a Minimum

If you want your teen to limit caffeine and avoid alcohol, it will help enormously for you to do likewise. If you get enough sleep, you won't need that second—or third—cup of a.m. coffee to come alive. And you definitely should avoid both coffee and tea at dinner and in the evening—they'll only keep you awake. I also suggest limiting nighttime alcohol to a glass of wine with dinner. Alcohol can interrupt your sleep, especially in the early morning between 2:00 and 5:00 a.m. It can also rev up emotions when you're trying to calm them down.

Don't Work in Your Bedroom

Does it drive you crazy to walk into your teen's room and see the bed covered with books, papers, clothes, and sports equipment? Do you wonder how your teen can relax and sleep with all that stuff everywhere?

The same might be asked about you. While many adults like to get into bed to work on their laptops or pay bills, it turns the bedroom into a work and activity area instead of a place for relaxation and sleep. You can set a good example by doing your work at your desk or on the dining room table and keeping your bedroom as a haven for relaxing and getting your ZZZZs.

Don't Overprogram Yourself

If you're stressed and not sleeping well, there's a good chance that, like many of us, you're completely overprogrammed. You work, raise your family, take care of your home and yard and pet, volunteer for several organizations, and on and on; there's little time to breathe, let alone relax. Not only is that bad for you, it can be damaging to your kids as well. It can take away from family time and it can lead kids to think that being busy every minute of the day is normal and that they should do it too. And that, as you probably know from experience, can make you stressed and interrupt your sleep.

As you work to support your teen, it may be a good idea to take a look at your own activity level. Then try to establish more realistic—and healthy—expectations for both of you.

Increase Your Family Time

As you take a look at your schedule, it may be a good time to consider how much time you, your spouse, and your kids spend as a family. If you're not together much, it can be difficult to share values, have experiences that keep you close, and simply enjoy the pleasure of each other's company. When home becomes a place just to coordinate

---

Another Parent Says . . .

❝I *work about nine hours a day, and then come home to making dinner, helping with homework, doing laundry, and paying bills. I also coach my daughter's soccer team, help out at church, work in the yard, and volunteer at Recording for the Blind. When my daughter started showing signs of exhaustion, I realized she was as overcommitted as I was. She gets up at 5:30 in the morning to go to religious school, then has high school classes till 3:00, soccer practice from 4:00 to 6:00, then dinner, homework, and helping me with her younger brother. On the weekends she has games and works at the local movie theater at night.* **❞**

calendars, the richness of life can get squeezed out and stress and dis-connection can squeeze in. It also becomes the norm for your children's future families.

To make room for family time, consider an all-house wind-down time. Listen to music together, play cards, or watch a relaxing video. Or set up a weekly family exercise time. Go for a run or a walk or work out on some home exercise equipment such as free weights or jump ropes. If your kids don't get hysterical watching you, put on some music and dance. Also try to have at least a couple of meals a week as a family.

IT'S A FACT

Eating together isn't just good for togetherness; it's also good for health and nutrition. A recent study detailed in the *Archives of Family Medicine* noted that children who have regular meals with their family eat more fruits and vegetables and less fat and fewer fried foods.

Follow Through

I talked earlier about the need to stick to your agreement and to enforce the consequences if your teen doesn't abide by the rules. But it's also very important to make sure that the whole treatment package is carried out. Not long ago I saw a teen and his mom and recom-mended that the boy use a light visor in the morning and take melato-nin in the late afternoon. At the follow-up visit a few weeks later, I asked the mom how the light treatments were going and she said, "Oh, we never got the visor. I didn't think it was that important." She never bought the visor and, surprise, surprise, her son's severe sleep delay was just as bad as ever.

Part of solving a sleep problem is taking the problem seriously. And part of taking things seriously is following through with treat-ment. Get a light visor if it's needed. Get a watch with an alarm if your teen needs a reminder to take her melatonin. Remember to recharge the light visor if you take on that responsibility. Call the family to dinner earlier if that keeps your teen from having trouble falling asleep on a full stomach. Commit to doing everything you can do to put all the recommendations in this book, and any recommendations from your teen's doctor, to work.

Keep Your Own Sleep Log

Keeping a log of your own sleep schedule and habits is a great way to see if you, like your teen, need to make a few changes. Do you routinely run a sleep deficit? Do you have trouble falling asleep most nights? Pinpointing any problems can get you on the road to solving them and give you some insight into what your teen is dealing with. You may also want to track how much caffeine and alcohol you take in and see what effect they're having on your ability to sleep well. For helpful information, you might also want to keep a sleep log for your teen, whether or not she's keeping one as well. Tracking all family members' habits will give you insight into the family dynamic.

Last but Not Least: Be Patient and Caring

A little restraint and a lot of love will go a long way in helping your teen become healthier and happier—and encourage your teen, I hope, to be patient and caring with you!

13

Making Changes in Your School and Community

Imagine this scenario: Your teen gets out of bed in the morning without you having to nag her and drag her out. She's in a pretty good mood, and there's no major hassle before she runs off to catch the school bus, with completed homework in hand. During first-period class and for the rest of the day, she's wide awake, participates in discussions, and even asks a question or two. When she gets back the chemistry exam she took a few days ago, she's gotten an A, a huge improvement from her usual grades in the sciences. After school, during track practice, she's full of energy and her coach tells her she's going to anchor the relay at the next meet. In the evening, though she's a bit tired after a full day, she does her homework, IMs with her friends, and gets to bed around 11:00. Before she drifts right off to sleep, she sets her alarm clock for 7:30 so she can get to school comfortably in time for her first class at 8:45.

Does this sound like a fantasy? If your teen, like most teens, has been grouchy, depressed, low performing, and often sick or energy deprived from lack of sleep, it may seem that way. But great days like this *can* become reality. (OK, her room's still a bit of a mess and she did get upset because the jeans she wanted to wear hadn't been washed, but this is as close to perfection as I can imagine.) All of the recommendations I've made so far will improve your teen's health, mood, performance, and well-being by helping her get more sleep. My final recommendation for making that happen, and it's a major one, is to get involved in the drive to move school start times later.

Having schools start just 45 minutes later can make a huge difference in your teen's life, because that can mean 45 minutes of additional sleep, with all the benefits sleep provides. (Contrary to what you might think, teens whose schools have later start times do use the extra time for sleep; they don't stay up later, but go to sleep at the same time they always have and sleep later in the morning.) After the high schools in the Arlington, Virginia, public school system moved their start times from 7:30 to 8:15 a.m., students reported in a survey that they felt more alert and prepared for school and teachers reported improvement in both student alertness and participation. Parents noted that their teens had a much better attitude. Other schools, one of whose journey to later start times I'll detail later, reported significant reductions in school dropout rates, less student depression, and higher student grades as well as a number of other extremely positive outcomes. Simply put, students who attend schools that are more in sync with their natural sleep-wake schedules are more able to learn and are happier doing it. Schools with later start times have positive effects on teachers and parents too.

IT'S A FACT

In a study of Minnesota schools in which start times were moved an hour later, results showed that:

- Discipline problems went down
- Illness calls dropped
- Grades trended up
- Student depression decreased
- Students and teachers were much happier

Could your teen and your area's schools benefit from later school start times? In a word, yes—and it's something both you and your teen can work toward. To help support your effort, this chapter is chock full of information and advice from organizations and schools that have made later start times a reality. You'll also find several ways to support sleep deprivation awareness in your schools and community.

Why We Have Early Start Times

Way back in the Dark Ages, when you and I were in middle school and high school, classes began somewhere around 8:15 or 8:30; my husband's school even began at 9:00. But over the last several decades, start times have crept ever earlier. According to the National Sleep Foundation, most high schools in the United States now start by 7:30 a.m., and some begin as early as 7:15. Because of shower and prep time; before-school activities, such as band practice and religious school; the need for parents to get their kids to school before they leave for the early work shift; and school bus schedules that are set in stone, many students now get up by 6:00 and some even at 5:00. That means many teenagers, whose circadian rhythm can keep them awake until midnight, are averaging no more than six hours of sleep a night.

What moved start times earlier? Basically, the financial straits that many schools are in. Districts with thousands of elementary, middle, and high school students to pick up and deliver found that it's far less costly for just a few buses and drivers to transport all the kids. So that means that some kids must be picked up very early, and therefore the schools must start early too. In Montgomery County, Maryland, high school students start boarding buses at 6:25 to be in class by 7:25.

The result of schools starting so early? As a recent study of the sleep patterns of incoming high school seniors, published in *Pediatrics*,

SNOOZE NEWS

In addition to contributing to sleep deprivation, which you now know results in myriad detrimental effects on teens' health and well-being, early school start times contribute directly to increased juvenile crime. According to the U.S. Department of Justice's Office of Juvenile Justice and Delinquency Prevention, violent crimes committed by juveniles peak in the hours right after school lets out; schools with early start times end on the early side too. The start of the day can present problems as well. Some students must get dropped off at school more than half an hour before classes begin, in order to give the buses time to pick up and deliver the other students. Often those students have minimal supervision, providing opportunity for trouble.

revealed, current high school start times contribute to sleep deprivation in adolescents. And as I've said throughout this book, sleep deprivation leads to many, many negative health, behavioral, emotional, and learning outcomes. Moving start times later, however, can help to turn those outcomes around.

School Districts That Have Made the Change

Because of all the information that's been surfacing on the relationship between teen sleep deprivation and poor school performance, school districts throughout the United States have been looking into the possibility of having later start times. Though a great deal is involved in making such a change, and while only a few districts have implemented the change as I write, the movement is growing and the results have been positive. Here is the story of one district that met the challenges and succeeded.

Wilton School District, Wilton, Connecticut

Wilton, Connecticut, is a suburban community with approximately 4,300 elementary, middle, and high school students. Before the start times were moved later, grades 3 to 5 began their day at 8:15, kindergarten to grade 2 began at 9:00, and grades 6 to 12 started at 7:35, with buses delivering the students at coordinated times.

The idea of having later start times came to the district through Wilton's League of Women Voters (WLWV), whose members had heard a presentation on the subject by the president of the Connecticut Senate, Kevin Sullivan. The League was intrigued, and put together a committee to investigate the issue further. Six months and a great deal of research and interviewing later, the committee presented its report and the WLWV decided to support later school start times. When the WLWV made its presentation, the superintendent of schools and the Board of Education were invited to attend. Both the superintendent and the board saw the benefits of the proposition, and quickly got behind the idea.

The WLWV then began to educate the public. Members spoke to as many community groups as they could, including the school PTAs. They also had a survey conducted that enabled students and teachers to contribute to a start time proposal. The Wilton Education Foundation provided an opportunity for the community to discuss the issue, and the Connecticut Thoracic Society assembled a task force to both raise awareness and advocate for the change.

Wilton's superintendent then announced that later start times would be put into effect. Parents were asked to provide input and meetings were held for questions and concerns. One big concern was the effect the new start times would have on the sports program. Many felt that the change in start times would negatively affect practices and games and cause Wilton to be dropped from its athletic conference. The other major concern was that younger children would have to start school earlier in order for the teens to start later.

After hearing the parents' concerns, the superintendent talked to the head of the athletic conference. The director agreed that later start times were important and said he would make every effort to work with the school's new schedule; he also promised that the district would not be dropped from the conference. The superintendent then decided that the youngest students, those in kindergarten through grade 2, should not be involved in the change and that no student should have to get on a bus before 7:00 a.m.

The superintendent next sent the proposed start times to his staff and the PTA. Though responses were mixed, he decided to send the proposal on to the Board of Education. In the spring of 2003, the board approved it.

In the fall of that year, the new schedule, which basically flipped the high school start time with the grade school start time, was put into effect. The upper elementary grades now started school at 7:35 and the middle and high schools started at 8:15, giving all the adolescents 40 more minutes of sleep.

What were the results of the change? For one, no additional buses had to be leased, so there was no increased transportation cost. Implementing the new schedule also went smoothly—it took administrators, parents, and students only about two months to adjust.

But the big changes were in high school student performance, behavior, attitude, and mood. A summary of the changes reported by the National Sleep Foundation noted that teachers found that students "were more awake, had better attitudes, and were overall more pleasant." In addition, the number of students who said they had no trouble with daytime sleepiness doubled and there has been a trend toward higher grades. Coaches at the school, who had been worried they wouldn't be able to hold practices because of the time change, reported that their teams had one of the best athletic seasons ever, winning several state championships.

A year after the later start time went into effect, the vast majority of the school community reported being very happy with the new schedule.

MORE POSITIVE OUTCOMES

Other high schools where the first bell now rings later, including the following, have also reported very positive results:

• In Minneapolis's Edina school district, studies found that there was marked improvement in student behavior, students felt more alert and well rested during the first hour of class and less tired at the end of the day, students had less erratic sleep behaviors, after-school activities were not negatively affected, there was a significant reduction in school dropout rates, less depression was evidenced, higher grades were reported, and teachers reported positive effects on both their professional and personal lives.

• In the Fayette County, Kentucky, school district, school attendance has gone up and tardiness is down. More than half the high school students in the district now get at least eight hours of sleep and the rate of traffic accidents in the county has gone down by 15 percent.

How *You* Can Help Change School Start Times

If, like many parents, you believe that having middle and high schools start later would benefit teen health and happiness, there's a lot you can do to support the effort at the local level.

First of all, you can educate your community on the difference in teens' circadian rhythm, the negative effects of sleep deprivation, how early start times contribute to sleep loss, and how teens do much better at schools with later start times. You may encounter opposition as you go— change scares a lot of people, and changes will have to be made—but try to network with people and organizations that support your position. Gather as many facts and positive examples as you can. Then make a plan for how you'll put your information to work.

The National Sleep Foundation's Web site (www.sleepfoundation.org), offers tons of information that will help you all along the way. The site provides fact sheets, information on a number of schools across the country that have succeeded in moving start times later, and ideas to consider as you go about designing your own plan and moving toward change. The organization also provides the following tips for making change more likely:

A TEEN'S TAKE

❝At 8:00 in the morning it is almost impossible to focus and take notes or a test without dozing off or thinking about how tired you are. If schools started later, teens wouldn't be constantly tired, allowing them to focus and accomplish so much more. They would perform better academically and physically. They wouldn't be so cranky and irritable. Basically everything would be better. ❞

- Start early to educate the community and all parties involved. Use hard data and testimonials. Consider the research and what you hope to gain, not lose. Network with other schools to learn from their experience. Apply what you learn to your school district's particular challenges or concerns.

- Community engagement is key, and this means parents, students, teachers, transportation staff, cafeteria staff, extracurricular personnel, coaches, employers, and anyone else involved in the issue. Understand from the beginning that a change in start times will affect the entire community, and set out to make sure that all of these parties are involved in the process. Involve them in a variety of ways (e-mail, letters, forums, surveys, etc.), and allow them the opportunity to express their opinions anonymously.

- Be clear about your goals. Keep your eye on the bottom line: the academic performance, health, safety, and quality of life for students. Do not get overwhelmed by the logistics and obstacles; rather, continue to emphasize the overall goal. Students' needs are foremost.

•   Be flexible as the process proceeds. Consider all the issues, needs, and agendas of all parties. Identify potential sources of resistance and address their needs. Be prepared with research and facts. Zealots generally are not effective.

•   Have a clear plan. Gather a coalition and form committees. Develop a timetable. Decide on guidelines for the change and create goals to measure your progress.

•   Communicate all along the way and especially throughout the implementation. Allow time to adjust and plan for the change.

THINK NATIONALLY AS WELL AS LOCALLY

Efforts to move school start times later are also happening at the state and national levels. Connecticut, Massachusetts, Nevada, and Virginia have introduced legislation to look into the issue. Though it hasn't yet passed, Congresswoman Zoe Lofgren of California introduced a resolution to the U.S. Congress to move school start times later. If you're interested in working to legislate wider change, a variety of federal agencies and national health care organizations, as well as social service organizations and parent-teacher associations, can help lead the way.

One Parent Group's Story

Despite the many challenges that can be involved, including transportation schedules and costs, after-school day care concerns for younger children, worries relating to after-school sports and other extracurricular activities, conflicts in facilities use, and related changes in teachers and parents' professional and personal lives, a number of school districts in several states have successfully moved school start times later. Other districts are now looking into the possibilities armed with facts and figures provided by parent groups and other organizations that have learned about the benefits the change could bring.

One of those parent groups is known as S.L.E.E.P., short for Sleep

Later for Excellence in Education Proposal. The group, whose goal is to move Fairfax County, Virginia, middle and high schools to later start times, was founded in 2003 by cochairs Phyllis Payne and Sandy Evans. Payne, a public health educator, and Evans, a journalist, were introduced by a mutual friend who knew of their common interest in the problems that stem from early school start times.

Phyllis Payne's interest in the issue actually started a number of years before she met Sandy Evans. Even though her own children were in elementary school at the time, she was concerned to see high school students waiting in the dark for the school bus every morning. Worried for them, she also projected ahead to when her own kids would have to wait in the dark. To all of that she added the fact that she wasn't an early riser, and looked ahead, with dread, to the time that she would be getting up well before dawn to get her own kids out the door.

As she thought about the problem, she began to read and learn more about it. She discovered that safety and what she calls "quality of life issues" weren't the only concerns. Because kids had to catch the bus so early, they had to wake up very early, most likely after going to sleep fairly late; teens were becoming sleep deprived, and sleep deprivation was harming them in a multitude of ways.

When Payne and Evans met, both had come to the conclusion that teenagers needed more sleep and that an important way to make that happen was to have schools start later in the morning. They also realized that sleep deprivation was a community-wide problem and that

SNOOZE NEWS

Still another way that sleep deprivation negatively affects teens is in what's called "school engagement," which the National Center on Effective Secondary Schools defines as being invested in and committed to learning. With as many as 40 percent of tenth, eleventh, and twelfth graders working 20 or more hours a week, and with teens' natural alert time being later in the day and in the evening, sleep researchers such as Mary Carskadon worry that a large number of students will come to prefer work, where they feel awake and good and are making money, over school. A study is now being done to look at the link between sleep loss, school engagement, and academic and emotional functioning in adolescents in order to foster greater school engagement. School engagement is especially important in urban areas because dropout rates tend to be higher there.

they needed to work for change not just for their own kids but for adolescents throughout the area.

The two started out by putting together a fact sheet about the effects of sleep deprivation and the benefits of later start times, and sent it to the Fairfax County Council of PTAs, seeking support. The response was immediate and positive. Payne and Evans received more than 300 e-mails from parents who knew the problems of sleep deprivation firsthand—and wanted to help.

The next steps the pair took were to create a Web site (www.sleepinfairfax.org) and start collecting signatures on a petition to start middle and high schools after 8:15 a.m. (the current start time for most of the high schools is 7:20; middle schools begin between 7:25 and 7:50). By putting the petition on the Web site, which a student helped design, they have been able to gather over 5,300 signatures so far, clear evidence of strong community interest in helping teens get more sleep.

Inspired by the outpouring of support, Payne and Evans have continued with their work. While the number of petition signatures grows, they have taken a sleep-related survey of students, teachers, and parents. They have also made presentations to school board members and to the superintendent of schools, both of whom determine the bell schedules for the district. The superintendent has already agreed to hire a transportation consultant to look into other possibilities for more effective use of buses and drivers. Evans has also done a route analysis of the buses in her area and found that 19 out of 22 buses pick up and deliver students to school in 38 minutes or less while three buses take an hour and 15 minutes. From this evidence, Evans and Payne believe that the students in those three buses, and other kids who spend a great deal of time on a bus, should be able to be transported to school in a much more reasonable time frame. They're now lobbying the school board and the superintendent for a route-by-route analysis.

When Payne and Evans founded S.L.E.E.P., they knew change wouldn't come easily. "Changes will have to be made, but it can be hard for some parents to imagine them, even when they know the end result will be good. Parents who don't have kids in middle or high school yet can have a particularly difficult time understanding the need," Phyllis Payne said. Dealing with the logistics involved with getting tens of thousands of students to 200 elementary, middle, and high schools on 1,500 buses was also daunting. Early on the pair learned that the school board had created a task force several years before to delve into the issue and that the task force hadn't been able to figure out an effective way to compress the bus schedules and make start times later.

Payne and Evans were encouraged to learn, though, that the task force had met only three times and that it had recommended the district keep trying to solve the problems, because later start times would benefit the entire community. They were also encouraged by the progress they were making and were determined to keep moving ahead.

Their goal, Phyllis Payne says, is to make start times later. But the way to that goal, she adds, is to educate and communicate—not propose a specific bus or school schedule. "Sandy and I aren't transportation experts," she states. "So we decided early on that it wasn't our job to come up with the solution. What we're trying to do is spread the word that there's a problem and that it can be fixed, and to get the entire community to work on the problem together. If we work school by school, each separate group will be trying to solve its own problems. That can lead to arguing and getting away from the real purpose.

"Everyone needs to know that last year the earliest bus pickup was at 5:45 a.m. This year it's 5:23. Some students are leaving for high school two hours before it begins, and they have that long ride home at the end of the day. Parents of younger kids don't know this is happening. Parents of kids who don't get picked up as early don't know it either. We want to inform the public and we want them to help us work for change."

But don't try to change things too fast, Payne advises. "People are so resistant to change, and if you try to move too quickly you're bound to fail," she states. "My daughter is in eighth grade now and my son is in fifth, and I do hope later start times will be in effect before they're out of high school. My goal, though, is to help have later starts for all the kids in the community."

MORE TIPS FROM S.L.E.E.P. TO START
A PARENT GROUP OF YOUR OWN

•   Find one volunteer at each of the high schools in your area to be a point person for outreach and to determine the problems at that school and those at its elementary and middle feeder schools. Those problems can then be brought to the attention of the main group.

•   If volunteers aren't available at some schools, look for student co-ordinators who are willing to help. Students can also act as adjuncts to adult volunteers.

•   Gathering signatures for a petition is easier and faster when done online. The Web site www.petitionsonline.com will let you establish one free of charge; you can make a donation if you like.

•   A short PowerPoint slide show is a great way to get the word out to administrators, PTAs, and others you want to reach. You can also connect with wider audiences by:

— Putting articles in parent newsletters and student newspapers

— Answering articles or letters to the editor about sleep and school start times

— Making up and distributing bumper stickers that include your Web site address (one of the S.L.E.E.P. stickers says "Tired of Early School Start Times?" and features the Web address)

— Linking your site to the PTA site

— Making presentations at Back to School Night and other events

•   Work with your school administrators. Some will resist the move for change but others will get behind it.

•   Recruit local college students to help compile data and to write reports.

•   Keep a file of all positive articles and data related to later start times and send copies to the superintendent of schools and all the members of the school board.

•   Network with schools in other districts where start times have been moved later.

Spreading Sleep Deprivation Awareness

As Phyllis Payne of S.L.E.E.P. said, above, it can take some time to see the drive to move school start times later succeed. But while that effort is going forward, there are several things you—and your teen—can do to get the word out about the detrimental effects of sleep deprivation.

• Encourage school administrators to include a unit on sleep in such classes as health, biology, or driver education. The National Institutes of Health provides a free supplementary curriculum on sleep aimed at ninth- through twelfth-grade biology students. The curriculum, entitled "Sleep, Sleep Disorders, and Biological Rhythms," is available in print form as well as online at www.science.education. nih.gov/supplements/nih3/sleep/default.htm. You can also work at the county or state level to have sleep education incorporated into the health curriculum in all elementary, middle, and high schools. Offer to arrange for a sleep doctor to speak at the annual meeting of science teachers to educate those teachers and have them become sleep advocates too.

• Encourage your teen to do a science fair project related to sleep. For example, she could track how much time friends, family members, and other students and adults sleep and how sleep duration and quality affect memory or reaction time.

• Talk with school administrators about holding a school wellness fair that includes a display about the benefits of sufficient sleep.

• Arrange for a sleep doctor from your community to speak to students, PTAs, or community forums.

• Develop fact sheets and obtain permission to distribute them to individuals or groups who work with teens, such as school nurses, coaches, and police personnel.

• Encourage your PTA to advocate for sleep deprivation awareness.

• Help younger children become aware of the negative effects of lack of sleep by working with local youth organi-

SNOOZE NEWS

Recently an exciting program was given the go-ahead to evaluate the effectiveness of a preventive sleep-education curriculum for middle schools. Funded by the National Institute of Child Health and Development, the Adolescent Sleep Smart Pacemaker Program will be tested with seventh graders over a three-year period. Developed by noted researcher Dr. Amy Wolfson, the eight-seminar course emphasizing the importance of sleep and good sleep habits may become the basis for integrating sleep education into our middle schools.

zations, such as the Girl Scouts and the Boy Scouts, to develop programs about sleep. Scouts could be awarded a badge for taking part in activities relating to sleep awareness.

• Once your teen has developed a successful sleep-wake regimen, encourage her to speak to friends and younger kids about strategies for getting more rest.

• Arrange an annual school assembly on sleep during National Sleep Awareness Week each March.

Part V

Global Impacts

14

Sleep Deprivation Around the World

Though the 24/7 culture of much of the United States certainly contributes to adolescent sleep problems, American teenagers aren't
the only kids who suffer the effects of sleep deprivation. Teenagers
across the globe find their natural circadian rhythms out of sync with
the people and places around them and find it difficult to get the quality and quantity of sleep they need to be their best.

Just as U.S. researchers are studying adolescent sleep issues in order to improve teen health, performance, and well-being, researchers
in most developed societies are delving into teen sleep patterns and
problems in their own countries. What are the results? Many studies
have shown that sleep deprivation and the effects associated with it are
common to adolescents no matter what their nationality. Differences
appear to arise only from cultural, socioeconomic, and environmental
factors.

One characteristic that teens in many countries have in common is
their night-owl behavior. Researchers Miriam Andrade and L. Menna-
Barreto found that 14- to 16-year-old Brazilian teens went to sleep
later on the weekends than 12- and 13-year-olds and that once adolescents reached puberty their sleep onset time became more delayed.
Studies in Australia, Japan, Italy, Finland, and Israel have reported
similar results.

A High School Student in England Reports . . .

❝My school, in London, starts at 8:30, but I have to get up at about 6:30 to get ready and to have enough time to take public transportation. I never feel like I really wake up until after my first double-period class is over at 9:45. When I stay up late on the weekends, which I usually do, I have a really hard time falling asleep on Sunday night and getting up Monday morning. On the weekends I can stay up till 3:00 a.m. and sleep till noon or 1:00. ❞

Many students in all the studies also reported increased daytime sleepiness. Just as in the United States, high schools in other countries start early in the morning—in Brazil they begin between 7:00 and 7:30 and in Israel at 8:00—leaving night owls exhausted as well as at risk for health and behavior consequences. According to researcher Amy Wolfson, teenagers in developed countries average a little over seven hours of sleep on school nights—a far cry from the eight and a half to nine and a half hours they should be getting.

What effects does this sleep deficit have on teens internationally? In China, a study of 1,538 adolescents revealed that regular nightly sleep of less than seven hours was significantly associated with increased behavior problems. In Italy, a study by Flavia Giannotti of 14- to 20-year-olds showed a correlation between increased daytime sleepiness, increased vulnerability to accidents, increased use of stimulants and tobacco, sleep problems, and anxiety. A survey of 1,457 Korean students revealed a progressive decrease in total sleep time from grades 5 to 12 of three hours on weeknights and one hour on weekends. Tenth graders averaged 6.02 hours of sleep on weeknights and twelfth graders just 4.86 hours. The study showed evidence of major detriments to functionality with symptoms of daytime sleepiness, depressed mood, and problem sleep-wake behavior.

Stress, just as it is in the United States, also is linked to sleep deprivation in other parts of the world. Israeli researcher Avi Sadeh has found that sleep is quite sensitive to emotions, expectations, and anxi-

A High School Student in Singapore Reports . . .

❝My high school starts at 7:20 a.m. It's so hard waking up in the morning. In first period class, which is reading, my friends and I all doze off while we're pretending to read. **❞**

eties and that the fatigue and sleepiness that result from sleep deprivation can actually become sources of stress themselves, creating a vicious cycle. In a study of the effects of trauma and stress from separation and loss, war and disasters, and child abuse on children's and adolescents' sleep patterns, he found that a 16-year-old girl was able to fall asleep easily only on the nights her older sister was home from military duty. When her sister was there, the two young women talked until they fell asleep. When her sister was away, the teenager took 40 minutes to fall asleep and then woke very early and couldn't get back to sleep. Her separation stress, and the related sleep difficulties, were helped by using relaxation techniques and leaving the radio on, set to shut off automatically later, as she went to bed.

IT'S A FACT

In a nationwide survey of close to 108,000 junior and senior high students in Japan, a significant relationship between short sleep duration and smoking was discovered. The study showed that 45 percent of daily smokers and 39 percent of occasional smokers slept less than six hours a night.

A Variety of Sleep Disturbances

What kinds of sleep difficulties do teenagers experience globally? As the above example points out, stress and anxiety often are associated with trouble falling asleep and trouble maintaining sleep. But all of the sleep disturbances American adolescents experience are seen in every developed nation. For example, a study by J. Vignau et al., reported in the *Journal of Adolescent Health*, found that more than 40 percent of

SLEEP THERAPY IN RUSSIA

In a program of lectures and workshops given in Russia, poor urban areas were shown to use a holistic approach to treating the growing problems of adolescent depression, high school dropout rates, and drug and alcohol abuse. Children and adolescents received massages and warm baths, acupuncture, various herbs, and rest during the day at sleep therapy clinics.

the French high school students surveyed had at least one of the problems being studied: difficulty falling asleep, difficulty staying asleep, needing more sleep, waking up too early, or chronically taking sleeping pills.

Another study, comparing the health of U.S. teenagers with teenagers in other countries, discovered similar sleep problems. The study, entitled the International Health Behavior in School-Aged Children Study, published as *U.S. Teens in Our World* by the U.S. Department of Health and Human Resources, asked 11-, 13-, and 15-year-olds in 29 countries a number of questions relating to their health. Two of those questions asked the students if they had trouble sleeping at least once a week and if they felt tired four or more times a week when they went to school. While U.S. boys ranked first in trouble sleeping and U.S. girls ranked second after France, both had rates similar to those of boys and girls in Canada, Wales, and Israel. About 40 percent of U.S. students said they felt tired in the mornings before school, boys slightly more than girls, but students in Norway and Finland ranked first and second, respectively, in that category.

SNOOZE NEWS

According to an article in the *Japan Times*, a global survey on sleep habits by market research firm A. C. Nielsen found that 41 percent of Japanese people get six or less hours of sleep a night, making Japan the most sleep-deprived country on earth.

Another study, of self-reported sleep problems among adolescents in Japan carried out by T. Ohida, showed a range of sleep difficulties among junior and senior high school students throughout the country. Between 15 and 39 percent of the students who participated had problems initiating sleep, slept less than six hours, or were excessively sleepy during the day during the previous month. The study concluded that sleep problems were common among Japanese adolescents. It also stated that being female, a student in senior high school, and having an unhealthy lifestyle, which included stress, smoking, and drinking alcohol, were risk factors for those problems. The study also concluded that there was a need for health education aimed at solving Japanese adolescents' sleep problems.

Cultural, Socioeconomic, and Environmental Differences Affecting Sleep

Though it's true that sleep deprivation and sleep disturbances are the bane of teenagers everywhere, different factors do contribute to the problems. For example, researchers who looked at data for a World Health Organization study of health behaviors, reported by Tynjala et al., found that teenagers slept longer in countries in which parents seemed to be stricter. A study of ethnocultural differences in the sleep complaints of adolescents in nine ethnocultural groups, performed by R. E. Roberts et al. and reported in the *Journal of Nervous and Mental Disease*, found that Chinese American teens had a significantly lower risk for insomnia than Anglo teens and that Mexican American teens had an increased risk compared to Anglos. African, Mexican, and Central American adolescents had an increased risk for hypersomnia, a condition in which a person sleeps excessively, and no group was at a lower risk for hypersomnia than the Anglo kids. The study suggested that minority status may affect the risk for sleep problems.

In Japan, which you've already read is a very sleep-deprived nation, hours in front of the TV as well as business pressures and social norms appear to be factors in people's lack of sleep. Many workers who put in long hours because of downsizing and restructuring often work well into the evening, then go out with colleagues for drinks, and then watch several hours of TV before heading for bed. A recent Eurodata TV Worldwide study reported that Japanese people average more than five hours a day watching television, more than people in any other country.

Here in the United States, an ongoing study at the University of Maryland may eventually provide data that could be applied worldwide. The study is examining the relationship between adolescent sleep-wake habits and daytime sleepiness as they relate to school engagement and academic performance in teens from varying racial and economic backgrounds in urban vs. suburban settings.

Summing It Up

Just what does this look at sleep around the globe tell us about worldwide sleep deprivation? From the data that's been gathered, it appears that adolescents in every developed country have the same problems with sleep that teens in the United States do, and that they're just as negatively affected by the resulting sleep deprivation. That's an alarming fact for both our teens and our world. Teens' lives are compromised now by the small amount of sleep they get and may be even more damaged as these adolescents reach maturity and start taking their places in the global community. And that state of affairs will keep our nations and our world from advancing to the greatest degree possible. The effects of sleep deprivation on today's teens—all 1.2 billion+ of them—may have significant and wide-ranging consequences in every corner of the world for years to come.

But taking the problem seriously now, and supporting efforts both locally and internationally to help teens get the sleep they need, will go a long way toward making teens' lives better today and all our lives brighter in the future.

Resources

Light Therapy Product Sources

Apollo Health
947 South 500 East, Suite 210
American Fork, UT 84003
(800) 545-9667
www.apollolight.com

Bio-Brite, Inc.
4340 East-West Highway, Suite 401S
Bethesda, MD 20814
(800) 621-LITE
www.biobrite.com

Enviro-Med
1600 S.E. 141st Avenue
Vancouver, WA 98683
(800) 222-DAWN
www.bio-light.com

Northern Light Technologies
8971 Henri-Bourassa West
Montreal, Quebec H4S 1P7, Canada
(800) 263-0066
www.northernlighttechnologies.com

Outside In, Ltd.
3 The Links, Trafalgar Way
Bar Hill
Cambridge CB3 8UD
England
+44 (0) 1954 780500
www.outsidein.co.uk

The SunBox Company
19217 Orbit Drive
Gaithersburg, MD 20879-4149
(800) 548-3968
www.sunboxco.com

Memory-Game Web Sites

www.miniclip.com

At this free game Web site, you'll find a great game to test memory
and reaction time. Tetris, a computer puzzle game that has been around
for several decades, asks players to move four-block shapes that are
falling into a well into a horizontal row of blocks without any gaps.
Players must rotate the shapes and complete as many horizontal lines
as possible before they reach the roof. You can change the speed at
which the shapes fall and use different strategies for getting the shapes
in line as quickly as possible.

The same site also offers a game called Anagrammatics. In this
game you click on letters to form words at least four letters long. The

idea is to find the longest possible words within the specified time limit. The site also offers the popular logic game called Sudoku. In this game you try to fill a puzzle grid so that every row, column, and 3 × 3 box contains the numbers 1 through 9.

www.memorylossonline.com

This site provides two memory tests (click on Memory Games), one for verbal memory and one for visual memory. The verbal quiz, which takes between 10 and 15 minutes, tests word memory, and the visual quiz, which takes about the same amount of time, tests picture memory. Each test has three parts, and at the end you're told what your score means and how you compare to other people who have taken the test.

www.gotofreegames.com

Playing the age-old game Concentration is another terrific way to test memory and performance. This Web site provides a 24-picture Concentration grid and times your play to see how quickly you can come up with the 12 matches.

www.jebikes.com/java/WhackAMole

This online version of the arcade game Whack-a-Mole, in which moles poke their heads up quickly and you have to whack them before they duck back underground, requires continuous attention and speedy visual reaction time. It's a way for your teen to assess sleepiness and possible microsleeps—and have fun at the same time.

Sleep-Related Organizations

American Academy of Pediatrics
141 Northwest Point Boulevard
Elk Grove Village, IL 60007-1098
(847) 434-4000
www.aap.org

American Academy of Sleep Medicine
One Westbrook Corporate Center, Suite 920
Westchester, IL 60154
(708) 492-0930
www.aasmnet.org

Better Sleep Council
501 Wythe Street
Alexandria, VA 22314-1917
www.bettersleep.org

National Center on Sleep Disorders Research
National Heart, Lung, and Blood Institute
One Rockledge Center, Suite 6022
6705 Rockledge Drive
Bethesda, MD 20892-7993
(301) 435-0199
www.nhlbi.nih.gov

National Highway Traffic Safety Administration
400 Seventh Street, SW
Washington, DC 20590
www.nhtsa.gov

National Parent Teacher Association
541 N. Fairbanks Court, Suite 1300
Chicago, IL 60611-3493
www.pta.org

National School Boards Foundation
1680 Duke Street
Alexandria, VA 22314
(312) 670-6782
www.nsbf.org

National Sleep Foundation
1522 K Street N.W., Suite 500
Washington, DC 20005
(202) 347-3471
www.sleepfoundation.org

S.L.E.E.P. (Start Later for Excellence in Education Proposal)
www.sleepinfairfax.org

Society for Adolescent Medicine
1916 N.W. Copper Oaks Circle
Blue Springs, MO 64015
www.adolescenthealth.org

Snooze . . . or Lose! Web Site

The *Snooze . . . or Lose!* web site includes additional information on adolescent sleep, Dr. Emsellem's speaking engagements, the opportunity to sign up for a newsletter, and contact information. Please visit us at www.snoozeorlose.com.

Acknowledgments

Thanks to my daughters, Stella, Nikki, and Elyssa, for providing me with the challenge of three very different, first-hand teen parenting experiences that allowed me to see sleep science in action and to fully appreciate the overwhelming need for this book. To Linda Croom, N.P., Karen Murtagh, N.P., and Erin Baehr, Ph.D., for treating adolescent patients with me, evaluating our treatment strategies, and helping to fine-tune our clinical approach. To Jessica Warburton, for spearheading our outreach program to bring our sleep message to the classroom. To my agent, Carol Roth, for her confidence in me, her tenacious determination to bring this book to parents and adolescents, and for recognizing the potential synergy with and introducing me to Carol Whiteley. To Carol Whiteley, for being the incredible writer she is and for so adeptly translating my lectures, theories, cases, and treatment strategies into this engaging book; there were times during this project when I truly believed that our thoughts were one. To Elaine Robertson, for the diagrams and illustrations that complement the text. To my adolescent patients, for helping me understand the challenges teens face, with special thanks to those who were willing to share their experiences for this book. To my editor, Jeff Robbins, and the staff of Joseph Henry Press for making my and Carol's words into this book.

Special thanks go to my daughter and contributing author Elyssa, for her eloquent commentaries and adolescent insights and for tolerating a sleep doc for her mom. And, finally, for standing by me throughout this project as an ever-present source of warmth and calm, thanks to my husband David.

Helene Emsellem

Snooze . . . or Lose! was created with the help of many talented, supportive people. My thanks go to my agent, Carol Susan Roth, of Carol Susan Roth Literary, for recognizing the importance of the book's subject matter and for working her magic to make the book reality. Thanks also to Helene Emsellem, sleep doctor extraordinaire, who made the writing of this book an adventure like no other. I also thank Phyllis Payne, co-chair of S.L.E.E.P., for her insights on how parents can effect later start times in their teen's high school. And special thanks go to the many young people who shared their thoughts about and experiences with sleep, particularly Elyssa Emsellem, Marlee Meikrantz, and Georgia Kleeman-Keller.

To my wonderful family, Mark, Trina, Bernie, and Jimmy, the biggest thanks of all.

Carol Whiteley

Index